LLADRÓ®

THE ART OF PORCELAIN

How Spanish porcelain became
world famous

SALVAT EDITORES, S.A.

Fotocomp. Llovet Fecha. 13,04,1984   Hora. 11.06 50
Directorio Nu.: 20
Nombre: D13/LLADRO INGL
Indice: FDV

Floppy 248

First Spanish printing: 10.000 exemplars
First English printing: 16.000 exemplars
Second English printing: 15.000 exemplars
Third English printing: 15.000 exemplars
Fourth English printing: 15.000 exemplars
Fifth English printing: 10.000 exemplars

© 1984 Salvat Editores, S. A. - Mallorca, 41-49
    Barcelona
ISBN: 84-401-0547-9
D.L.B.-6.311-1984
Printing: IHASA - Mallorca, 51 - Barcelona, 1984
Printed in Spain

Collaborators

Foreword:
ROBERT J. CHARLESTON

The Lladró Brothers; Three Personalities
and a Single Work:
NESTOR LUJAN

Genesis of a Lladró Porcelain Work of Art:
MAURICIO WIESENTHAL

Aesthetics and Themes in Lladró Porcelain:
JORGE PLAYA, ARNAU PUIG, MARCIAL OLIVAR

English Version:
RICHARD LEWIS REES

Photographs:
CARRAZONI
JAIME COSTA
ANTONIO MURILLO
ALICIA NOE

Designer:
FERRAN JAVALOYES

Contents

Foreword

The setting up of a successful porcelain manufacture in post-war Europe is no mean achievement under any circumstances. To do so with very limited capital resources is doubly remarkable. This, however, is what the brothers José, Juan and Vicente Lladró have done. The first two trained at art college as painters and the last-named as a sculptor, and when in 1951 they started operations in Almácera with a wood-fired furnace such as would have been used by their moorish predecessors in medieval Valencia, they were at first constrained to exercise their talents on making the ceramic flowers which continue to play an important role in their production. An interesting comparison with the early days of the French factory at Vincennes which later became the royal manufacture of Sèvres, and where porcelain flowers formed to some extent the bread-and-butter line of its early production.

As the Lladró concern prospered, with an outlet in Valencia in 1955 and a new factory at Tabernes Blanques in 1958, it began to present the extremely rare aspect of a concern which concentrated almost exclusively on its production of ceramic figures, at the expense of those utilitarian wares which normally provide the backbone of a ceramic factory's commercial success. There are very few historical parallels indeed for such a state of affairs, and the emphasis reflects very much the predominantly sculptural sympathies of the three brothers who provide the driving-force of this remarkable enterprise. The painting side, however, is by no means neglected, and most of the figural work is painted, often in washes of pastel colours which have been developed in the factory's own laboratory. The creation of a whole range of porcelain figures has always been a testing assignment for any ceramic factory and the making of a porcelain figure is by no means as simple an act as the finished result might suggest.

Not all sculpture can be automatically transposed into porcelain, and the most successful porcelain modellers of the past have been those who were able to visualise the effects of modelled surfaces when they are covered with brilliant reflective glaze. The Lladró team well realise this, and the details of modelling are often smoothed out in order to give simple surfaces on which the glaze will tell. Against these broader effects the relatively busy details of flowers and the paraphernalia of basketwork which was the pride of the Belleek factory provide a marked contrast.

The subject-matter of a range of porcelain figures inevitably poses limitations. This is not a medium which encourages heroic proportions, and indeed the technical difficulties of firing large porcelain figures and groups have always daunted the makers. This, however, is not the main reason why porcelain figure-making has always inclined to the miniature. A large sculpture which might look well with a surface of natural clay would look very different when given a covering of glistening light-reflecting glaze. Even J. Kändler, the great modeller of the Meissen factory, who was the virtual creator of the European porcelain figure, was less than entirely successful with the life-size animals and birds which he made for the adornment of the Japanese Palace in Dresden, let alone the overlife-size equestrian figure of the Elector Augustus II which he projected but never completed. Nor did F. A. Bustelli, his brilliant rival of the rococo period at Nymphenburg, succeed much better. His bust of Count Sigmund von Haimhausen, although immensely impressive, is not wholly successful as a work of art. The art of the porcelain figure, therefore, is essentially that of the miniature, and solemn themes and monumental forms do not lend themselves easily to miniature treatment. It follows that porcelain figures tend to be used for domestic, sentimental and decorative themes.

Kändler and Bustelli both cultivated the gay subject-matter of the Commedia dell'Arte, and Harlequin has never ceased to appeal to the porcelain-modeller. The Lladró Harlequin, however, has a cast of melancholy totally different from the spirit of Kändler's creations, and a mood which is not common in porcelain. In this, as is natural in a Spanish context, he is joined by Don Quixote himself, equally lean and tall. This tendency to elongation of the figure is indeed a noticeable feature of the Lladró repertory, as in those figures representing characters of the ballet, or sportsmen out shooting, or a mother with child.

Children here play a great role. Not the chubby impersonal *putti* of a Bustelli, but children in all their domestic aspects. Little girls trying on hats, little sentimental girls with lambs, or boys with donkeys. There are girls with cats and girls milking, and little goose-girls, painted in washes of cool grey and beige reminiscent of those used by the royal Copenhagen factory, in whose repertory some of these figures would not look amiss. A real feeling for childhood makes itself evident in these figures, and there is an affinity with the work of past modellers for whom these qualities had a special appeal. Artists like J. P. Melchior, of the Hochst factory, so many of whose figure-subjects drew on the theme of childhood. There are also elegant girls of a more advanced age, sitting on a bench, leaning on a balustrade, or swinging on a swing out of Fragonard.

The world of the theatre, which for Kändler had meant the Commedia dell'Arte, here also embraces Shakespeare: groups of Romeo and Juliet or Othello and Desdemona enveloped in a certain atmosphere of solemnity, and a Hamlet, skull in hand, full as melancholy as the Harlequin and the Don Quixote.

A vein which was well-worked in Italy produced themes which perhaps crossed the sea when the Capodimonte factory transferred to Buen Retiro. These were subjects drawn from everyday life, to be seen here in the figure of an old man with his dog, the archetypal image of the figure from low life, at one with the Contadini of Doccia or

Capodimonte, but perhaps inspired by one of those
bearded patriarchs from the lower orders of society
portrayed so sympathetically by Velasquez himself?

Set somewhat apart from these themes, already
for the most part well-known among the subjects
of European porcelain figure-modelling, are others
of which the 18th century could hardly have known.
The Turks and Chinese of Meissen have their
counterparts here in the groups of Eskimo children
or the Balinese dancers. Curiously enough, these
figures seem to show a tendency to develop in other
ways. There is a departure from the pastel colouring
with which the more traditional types of figures
are treated, in favour of terracotta browns and reds,
seen again in a robust study of a girl holding
a pitcher which displays a certain roughness
of texture alien to most of the figures already
alluded to. Is it perhaps possible to discern in this
a new direction in which this remarkable factory
might strike out leaving behind the legacy of the past?

R. J. Charleston, M.A., F.S.A.;
Formerly Keeper of the Department
of Ceramics, Victoria
and Albert Museum, London.

The Lladró Brothers: Three Personalities and a Single Work

Four kilometres from Valencia, and scarcely two from the sea, Almácera is a typical small town of the Valencian *huerta:* fertile, cultivated land, particularly in the provinces of Valencia and Murcia. The politician and geographer Pascual Madoz, in his "Diccionario Geográfico Estadístico-Histórico de España y sus posesiones de Ultramar" an erudite and extensive work full of information and curiosities published between 1845 and 1850, describes with precision the features of this town where "no finer more intensely cultivated earth could be found (...) rich, as it is, with a multitude of trees of different species and different kinds of seed-beds; it has all kinds of fruit in never-ending supply, each more succulent than the next, so that the inhabitants' diligent labour and constant dedication to agriculture are fully rewarded". And he adds that "All the four winds vie freely with each other for supremacy in Almácera; its sky is joyful, and the atmosphere most clear". It is known that the origins of Almácera go back to the time of the Moslem domination. Islamic culture stretched then from fantastic Bagdhad to the Hispanic Peninsula where it left its cultural and artistic legacy. Consequently Almácera was Arab until Jaime I conquered it and donated it to the Bishop of Huesca, Vidal de Canyelles.

Water, earth, a clear and transparent atmosphere, luminosity, in sum, vitality, define this town whose characteristics have persisted through the centuries.

Almácera has always been an agrarian town and, alongside its neighbour Alboraya, a major producer of the chufa, or earth-almond, so well-known in the Middle Ages and for which the latter town is the principal trading centre. The people of both Almácera and Alboraya not only left town to sell them in the capital, Valencia, but also, in the words of Pascual Madoz, at Court, "where they were used in the summer months to make 'horchata' or other refreshments known by the name of *chufas*". Consequently Almácera was not just a town of agriculturists but also of traders who departed adventurously from their whitewashed towns and their tenaciously cultivated fields to sell their products with an enthusiastic capacity for iniciative. They were the ideal people to carry out such enterprises.

* * *

It was on these luscious and irrigated lands that three brothers were born, Juan, José and Vicente. They came from peasant stock and were the sons of Juan Lladró Cortina and Rosa Dolz Pastor, the former native of Almácera while his wife hailed from Alboraya. The father —who is still living and is

Principal façade of the Lladró porcelain factory in Tabernes Blanques, Valencia. This attractive building cleverly combines the wings where the art and production departments are housed with the spectacular central pavilion of the Administrative Offices, and the Exhibition Hall of Lladró porcelain.

_____

* Died in 1981, after the first edition of this book.

a magnificient specimen* of the timeless and noble 'huertano' of Valencia— was a day-labourer constantly in touch with the earth, working it with that profound conviction of the man who loves an essential and rigorous task. And he transmitted this feeling for his work to his sons, who became labourers themselves while still practically infants. Their mother, as uncomplicated as she was intelligent, was able to imbue each and every one of her sons with a fine sensitivity for small things —those that make great things possible—, inculcated them with a great sense of responsability and was at

They knew that from such earth a new, exciting world, could be brought to life. They knew that their hands were of the earth and for the earth and, sure of their vocation, they burned many nights of midnight oil to combine their work with their studies of the plastic arts.

The Valencian's love for painting, sculpture, drawing and the artesan's craft has been commented upon a thousand times. Alongside this colourful and spectacular artistic vision of life, however, exists a knowledge of the secrets of the purely terrestrial kingdom. The Valencian, as Théophile Gautier said of himself, is a man for whom the exterior world exists. This apparently meaningless paradox is absolutely true: the exterior world exists to be constantly recreated, to be seen through new eyes, to be modelled by new hands, to be painted with new brushes. Thus the earth surrounding the Lladró brothers, apart from its fertility and fruitfulness, gave them the idea of its plasticity, its malleable qualities allowing it to be shaped into a thousand different forms reproducing movement, beauty, life.

Their first years of school meant bitter sacrifices for them, each one of the brothers contributing hours of toil in the family fields to make their economic situation more tolerable. Juan Lladró Dolz felt his vocation very early on in life; at the age of fourteen he entered the Escuela de Artes y Oficios de San Carlos where he studied line drawing, design and ceramics. He was able to assimilate the teachings of his tutors: José Contreras, José Américo and Enrique Navas (design); Santiago Rodríguez García (history of art); Manuel Diago, the great fan painter (decorative composition); Enrique Bellido (line drawing) and Alfonso Blat, director of the Manises school, who was his initiator into ceramics. With his knowledge, and under the direction of Vicente Bertrán, he became first official painter and began his artistic activities in the world of porcelain. The road undertaken by Juan Lladró was soon followed by his brother José. They were both to share labours in the family fields, the modest school and the simple but valuable experiences offered them by their work as apprentices in the Azulejera Valenciana (Valencian Tile Factory) and which encouraged them to register for night classes in the Escuela de

all times for them a model example of abstinence and constancy. The seed planted with such sacrifice would later give forth magnificent fruits.

The three brothers are native of Almácera: Juan, the eldest, was born on June 6 1926; José on January 3 1928; and Vicente on March 5 1933. From their earliest infancy their father taught them to cultivate and to love the land. He taught them to appreciate not only the value of its fertility but also its quality as a plastic material, which could be felt in the hands and shaped into the recondite, hard and fragile beauty of porcelain.

Artes y Oficios de San Carlos, in Valencia. They were eight years of sacrifice comprehensible only in the light of the firm determination which is characteristic of them today and which they already possessed then.

José Lladró's teachers were José Bellver and Vicente Gil (design); and the painter and decorator Francisco Sebastián, besides those who had already seen his brother Juan through his formative years.

His sojourn through the Escuela de Artes y Oficios was marked with deserved and high distinctions. As did his brother, José painted in oils and water-colour, decorated fans and thought up publicity posters and it was from this constant and enthusiastic common labour that the two brothers had the idea of starting their own workshop.

The youngest brother, Vicente, was fired by the same artistic vocation. It was perhaps he who became most deeply rooted to his native earth, which he cherishes with a profound instinct. At the age of fourteen he was already helping his father in his tasks and, running away from the house one day, won an 'upright ploughing' competition. He, like his brothers, had since adolescence the classic obsession for the ''work well done'', finished with the same precision with which it was conceived. In his case, however, the artistic vocation was felt as much in the hands as in the retina, and he decided to become a sculptor.

Like his brothers he entered the Escuela de Artes y Oficios de Valencia at the age of fourteen and, despite the attempts of Salvador Tuset, a painter who had been a disciple of Sorolla and who was professor of coloration, to persuade him to become a painter, he was determined to sculpt. Consequently he attended classes by Roberto Rubio. As a sculptor he was soon to learn all the difficulties as well as the peculiar pleasures of creating form and movement. It is hardly surprising, then, that

these three essentially hard-working brothers, ambitious in the most legitimate sense of the word, should decide to create a collective work, a family entity which over the years has come to symbolize all the industriousness of the creative Valencian people who have given the region its characteristic vigour.

En 1951 they decided to begin the enterprise despite the seemingly insuperable economic difficulties this involved. With a tenacity stronger than any adversity they overcame the first problem, constructing a kiln in the patio of their house in the Calle de San José. They took as their model the typical Moorish kiln, which burned the wood indigenous to the low Valencian hills, rosemary and gorse, and which reached temperatures suitable only for firing ceramics.

Today it is odd to think of these three young men from Almácera suffering all kinds of vicissitude with their inadequate means. They began by making little floral decorations for lamps manufactured by a specialized industry. These lamps are easily brought to mind thanks precisely to the delicacy and personality of the decorative flowers. All three brothers modelled them; then the two elder ones carried out the decorations while the youngest did the firing.

It is highly significant that floral decoration should be the first task of these Valencian founders of a veritable industrial empire of artistic porcelain. Flowers spring immediately, and from time immemorial, to any Spaniard's mind when Valencia is mentioned, when he pictures her wonderful gardens and her ancient and delightful *ruzafas* (garden-parks).

21

Vicente Lladró contemplating some of the works created by his own hands. The outstanding Sèvres-type vase was made by the three brothers together and has become the symbol of their combined efforts.

Those first diminutive flowers attracted the first customers and the beginnings of economic possibility and, since the demand was great, the brothers acquired techniques of perfecting them in a spontaneous yet gentle manner. Today flowers still play an important rôle in the decoration of all Lladró porcelain; they are a constant, fragile and delicate presence. When the necessity to increase their output arose, they brought in some of the girls from the town and taught them the beauty of flower modelling. The girls would make the models and the brothers would then decorate and fire them. This meant that from the very beginning feminine hands, ingenuous, delicate, indefatigable and largely anonymous, played a highly important part in these works: an importance which continues to this day in the extensive catalogue of the Lladró workshops where each of the varieties, conceived with such patience, constitutes in itself a veritable artistic school. Then came the possibility of possessing a very rudimentary kiln —built from the remains of bricks thrown out from the Altos Hornos (High Kilns) at Sagunto— capable of producing the degree of glazing suitable for porcelain. And from the moment they first handled porcelain they have been unable to put it down; it has become an obsessive adventure in the life of these humble men born to work the earth, not to create from it. But porcelain is a delicate passion. Let us not forget that during the eighteenth century all European sovereigns vied with each other in its manufacture: it was one of the exquisite crazes of that most refined of centuries. Workers were stolen, almost kidnapped, great painters contracted and the technicians given noble titles. Those royal enterprises from the age of enlightened despotism, with all the wealth of equipment and talent the absolute monarchs had at their disposal, have been reproduced in twentieth-century Valencia, and the three brothers, born in the Calle de San José in Almácera, have

surpassed in output all the most traditional workshops. They have been unable to shake off their obsession since the very beginning, when they made vases in the style of Dresden or Sèvres, when Vicente modelled the children who adorned them and his brothers decorated them with pastoral or chivalrous scenes.

But, as one would expect, this was not what they wanted to do, nor could they limit themselves to an imitative style which, in any case, had little to do with contemporary sensitivity and taste. Thus appeared all the themes and stylizations which over the years have simply reaffirmed themselves: ballerinas, flowers, figures of dancers, little boys playing delicately amongst themselves or caressing small animals. An enthusiastic team of collaborators, skilfully trained by the Lladró brothers, help them advance through their various epochs. Like the brothers they are simple, hard-working people, but conscious that theirs is important work, that their hands "create" works apparently anonymous, but that as a team they are bringing wonderful miracles of art to life. Juan, with his ever-critical spirit, demands accuracy and elaborate delicacy in the making of a piece of porcelain; by his side, José and Vicente apply themselves to putting the finishing touches to more and more complicated pieces, try out new types of kilns or study the arrangement of pieces inside them. Each year brings new challenges, new technical difficulties to be overcome; but it is from this very process that the "Lladró style" evolved and continues to evolve. When today we wander though the spacious naves of the modern factory, it is not difficult to recognize many of those who made these advances possible, and we remember the names of Agustín Bertomeu, Angelita Cabo, Amparo Escorihuela, Manuel Hurtado, Julia Laparra, Manuel Leonor, José Marí, Vicenta Montañana, Juan José Peris, Ricardo Peyró, Miguel Ramón, Ramón Ribes, Amparo Valero and Manuel Valero, among others.

Then, in 1955, they opened a shop in Valencia and within a few years economic difficulties had been overcome. In the blinking of an eye, the three brothers had become not only artists but also businessmen. Suddenly they had to do everything at the same time, and the demands of progress and industry obliged them to convert their tiny

family workshop into a factory. Three years later, in 1958, the foundations for their first factory were laid in the neighbouring town of Tabernes Blanques. They began to gather new collaborators around them, organizing highly specialized departments which attracted a whole team of men with unparalleled experience in the field of artistic porcelainware. But this is not the place to analyze the work, the artistic direction or the scientific or industrial weight of the "Lladró complex" which employs more than two thousand people and sells its products in almost one hundred countries. What concerns us here is the personality of the three businessmen who, along with professor Antonio Valero Vicente, form the Board of Directors of one of the most astonishing industries in the world, made possible by the capability and enthusiasm of each of its members, in particular the efforts of its main directors Vicente Oltra, Manuel Moure, Ramón Ribes, Alberto Ramón, José M.ª Alcalá, Francisco Varea, Julia Laparra, Juan José Peris and Amparo Tuset, who continue to modernize porcelain techniques, sales procedures and who have successfully managed to introduce their works of art practically the whole world over, forming a team with the Heads of Departments.

Above all, the secret lies in a profound love for their work. I remember having read somewhere that the French sculptor, August Rodin, when encountering a close friend, would greet him with, "Have you worked well?" And if the other replied in the affirmative Rodin's mind was set at rest and he needed to ask no more. For Rodin, he who worked well was happy and work was something as simple, as uncomplicated and as natural as living. The key to these extraordinary peoples' success, to my way of thinking, lies in this enthusiasm

The Lladró family with their original collaborators outside the house at No. 7, Calle de San José, in Almácera, the family home which saw the beginnings of the present-day industrial complex.

with the spirit of men given over to a satisfying destiny: humility, constant dedication and supreme joy.

The key to success lies obviously in this will to work, but it is also to be found in that rare spiritual equilibrium I have observed in the three brothers. In other words, in the satisfaction given them by a creative task with which they are entirely in tune, by industrial capacity which is satisfactory enough to give employment to so many people, by their commercial good-sense which assures them constant, almost astonishing success and, finally, by the profound pride in having achieved success, renown and, above all, a personal style known throughout the whole world.

Each one of the brothers reveals this equilibrium differently. Juan is the one who appears to have it most, in a reflective way. This means that, besides his constant search for new forms, he is interested in research, method and science. His eyes are constantly on the lookout for new discoveries: a line, a colour, a shadow. Nature, people, landscape, all rivet his attention through the open window which is life for many people, that window beside which he loves to sit when travelling by air or by rail. He is an amiable man, somewhat introspective at times, as if by looking outwards he were trying to look inwards, in a desire not to waste time. Time is a constant challenge to him in his work: it is as if his whole life has been a battle against time in a determination not to squander it. His tight journey-schedules, his contacts with clients and collectors who seek his autograph on the pieces in their possession, do not prevent his taking time off, when he hardly disposes of any at all, to see monuments, museums and collections in the cities he visits. He is one of those rare people who possess supreme self-confidence along with sufficient spiritual elegance not to show it. Behind his courtesy one can detect a vital energy, an acute critical sense which confers upon him a formal aggressiveness which might surprise those who know him only superficially, and which contrasts with the ever-alert clarity of his judgements and words.

for day-to-day work. I have known all three of them and I believe that if any one had to ask a person dear to him if that person is happy, he would ask, as did the French sculptor, whether he was working well and, similarly, if he had to ask if his health was good, he would ask if he had been able to work to his entire satisfaction. Because the idea of happiness is to be able to work and men who have created something important have considered health as that ability to work in the same way as Nature does, with a noble and serene breath. It is to work as Lope de Vega did,

Stylization, thematic variety, colour, technical quality and painstaking care in the execution of the different tasks are all constants which define the so-called Lladró style.

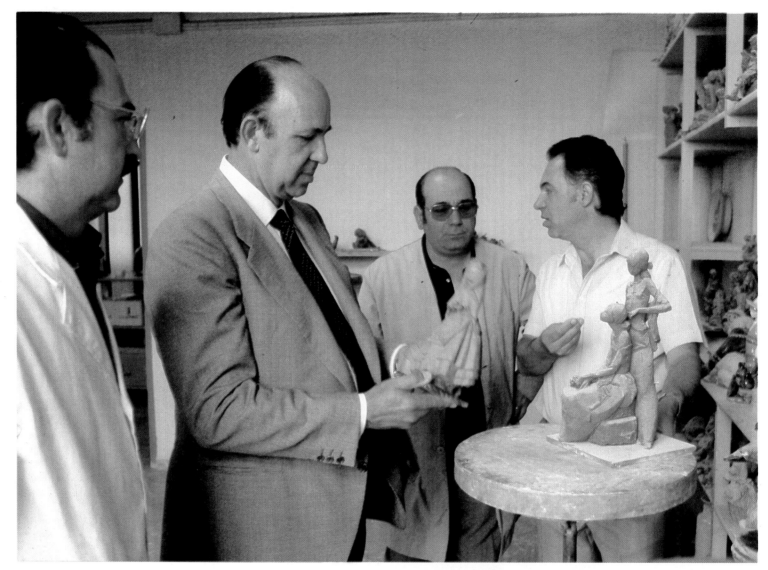

In the above photograph and on the following page we see the Lladró brothers discussing future projects. Here they count on the collaboration of the sculptors and decorators Antonio Ballester, Francisco Catalá, Salvador Debón, Julio Fernández, Salvador Furió, Juan Huerta, Vicente Martínez and Julio Ruiz. On the right: Juan Lladró in the firm's Chemistry Department whith a few of his collaborators, among them Rosario Boix, Ramón Gil, Claudio Guillem, Antonio Molina and Adolfo Pucilowski.

Examples of perfect symbiosis, the Lladró brothers combine their artistic and creative activities with the high responsability of company administration.

Physically José represents what he is spiritually: he is the tallest of the three, robust, and one sees in him the innate organizer, the imaginative one who is probably the key to the whole structure of the enterprise. He has the full, broad vision of the coordinator and the restlessness of someone who plans for the future. His openness and his important yet benevolent mien do not lack an air of authority and evidence of that vital fluid which emanates from those who make plans for the things they know and love. Surrounded by practically irreplaceable friends and collaborators, many of whol today carry out activities and tasks initiated by him, he exercises an affectionate tutorage over them which keeps him from losing touch with all the different facets of the work. This apparent accumulation of functions in his person is effaced by his cordial treatment of all who work with him. If Juan's life revolves around time, then José's has its foundations in work, work and business sense. These are the two essential components in the life of this man, alternating with trips all around the world to greet clients and friends, and short holidays on the Valencian beaches or in the nearby mountains. A man of great sensitivity, he cultivates the friendship of all those in contact with him. It is certainly true that in this sense the three brothers are totally linked to the people who collaborate with them. It is a kind of ancient and indefinable brotherhood, an essential, gentle fraternity so obviously

there despite its lack of external formulation. It springs from long generations of men who work together in the industrious, vital towns of Valencia, this region which history has never managed to subdue.

In Vicente, the youngest, this supreme quality of belonging to the people is at its most acute. But then we also have his own personality: he is the sculptor, the man made to touch realities. And he does so with such generosity one could almost call it total self-denial. His contribution is one of enthusiasm and strength. He lives intensely the life of Almácera and he shares it with whoever works with him. One senses that he is irreplaceable, as much in the

*Left: interior view of the Central Pavilion. Above:
Board of Directors formed, from left to right, by
Vicente and Juan Lladró, professor Antonio Valero
Vicente and José Lladró, and the company solicitor,
Alberto Ramón.*

human relations inside the factory as in
those outside. His interest in facing even the most
trivial problems, sometimes with exaggerated fervour,
is offset by the way he always solves them, be they
great or small, a quality which makes him
indispensable at decision-making time, and he
carries with pride his personal importance as a
director. His trips to national and international
Fairs and his work as a director are interrupted
momentarily only when he goes to the mountains,

rifle over his shoulder, to hunt small game, or
when he immerses himself in the sport of civil
aviation. Vicente, like his brothers, began
working with his hands, those hands which the
poet Rainer Maria Rilke described as a subtle
and complicated organism, like a delta into which
flows a life which comes from far away to pour
itself into the great torrent of action. An
appropriate image for this world where hands are
essential for these industries and these arts.
From the feminine hands of little girls or near
adolescents who model the flowers or paint the
rainbow colours of a bird, to those sensitive and
powerful hands which control the enterprise
and which contain, materially and spiritually, that
superhuman energy which has made the Lladró

33

View of the installations where the competitions and sporting activities take place. This facility for the great family which is the Lladró company, along with artistic and advertizing training programmes, is an example of the social works under the care of Amparo Tuset.

factory one of the most important of its kind in the world, thanks to its never-ending fountain of invention and its industrial importance.

Three men united also by the sacrifice of their wives, three Valencian women who have preferred to renounce just human aspirations in favour of business: Dolores Sala, native of Valencia and married to Juan; Carmen Castelló, born in Tabernes Blanques, José's wife, and Amparo Roig, from Almácera, married to Vicente.

Three personalities, three extremely cordial people who are easily approachable, and whose secret lies probably in their equilibrium and sense of proportion: the spiritual equilibrium between a great enterprise and the sensitivity needed to carry out the daily development of an art they have created, of a style which has achieved great acclaim not only in their own

country but all the world over. Three men essentially open and uncomplicated yet possessing an astonishing multiplicity of qualities, personalities and impulses. And this happy multiplicity has crystallized, harmonized, complemented and even supplemented itself into a determination never to weaken the union between them or the unity of action of the enterprise, subordinating personal criteria to the better functioning of the whole. This unanimous, full and rich undertaking, perhaps unique in the varied and impressive history of porcelain, is simply the logical result of a series of actions on both a personal and commercial level which, nevertheless, pass unnoticed by our present-day society which ignores most things of real importance. For once, however, the efforts of a team of directors and the enthusiasm of thousands of collaborators have made this reality possible, one more step along the way to the future "city of porcelain", the pride of Valencia and of Spain.

Genesis of a Lladró Porcelain Work of Art

Man, in his desire to communicate and to perpetuate himself, has built many monuments: the pyramids of Egypt, the Great Wall of China, the Acropolis of Athens. From Persepolis to Manhattan, the world is full of declarations of strength, pride and faith.

History, like the actors of ancient Greek theatre, likes to present itself in this way, behind a grandiloquent disguise. However these great constructions are somewhat dramatic and insincere: with their masks they hide from us the intimate sentiments of the men who created them. The archaeologist knows that one must always seek out the heart of history; one has to search beneath the disguise in order to discover its real identity. Many civilizations, proud of their great monuments, have become immortalized in the end thanks to their "minor arts". This is the case of, for example, Imperial China which has come down to us thanks to its delicate arts of silk and porcelain. Few monuments could rival the grandiose constructions built by those refined and idle emperors who lived enclosed within great walls. Nevertheless they became famous thanks to a series of "trivialities": tea, spices, silk fabrics and those translucent porcelain pieces which Marco Polo compared to the mother-of-pearl of a small mollusc called *porcella.*

The Lladró brothers have managed to discover the secrets —not only technical but also philosophical— of these ancient "minor arts"; they have penetrated beyond the dramatic disguise of history to discover that intimate truth which beats in the tiny heart of objects; they have converted dust into porcelain, clay into art, material into beauty. And often, when Spain is mentioned in the United States, Australia or Great Britain, not only do people speak about the Escorial or the Inquisition but also a delicate type of porcelainware which displays a tenderer, deeper concept of the life of Spaniards. This is, perhaps, one of the paradoxes of history; that in the tourist brochures the great things are mentioned, but the visitor, when he comes, is taken by simple things: rustic craftsmanship, fabrics or porcelain. These are Spain's best embassies.

Great works die young, like romantic heroes. Only the small crafts of the spirit prevail, like those wise lives which are ennobled by the passing years.

How is a work of art created?

When we enter a craftsman's workshop we commit a fascinating indiscretion; it is like penetrating the intimacy of a soul. The enchanted legend of art and life can so easily be smashed beneath the chisel-blow of analysis. Art is a miracle, it should appear as a miracle and it should always be contemplated with loving eyes.

The creative process begins with the sketch where characteristics of position, movement and size are studied, and is brought to fruition at the modelling stage in which the figures acquire volume and are delicately sculpted in their minutest details.

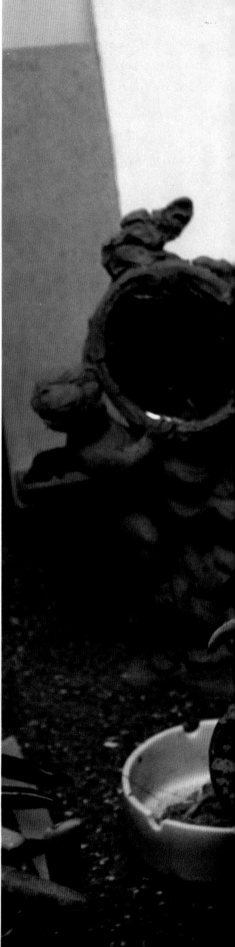

We enter the craftsman's workshop, then, with a certain misgiving, because porcelain pieces do not admit a brutal analysis and can suddenly be destroyed, like mistreated lives.

We go to see them, indiscreetly, at the moment of their creation; we are going to surprise them naked and sad, melancholy and without makeup. Perhaps we shall learn to know them better, but in the long run we shall love them for their mystery and their legend, as if they were the offspring of a fascinating and ingenuous miracle.

A whole team of specialists, working in perfect harmony, goes to create a work of art. The sculptors make a sketch and discuss with the painters any problems of colour; they also make a model. The chemists (would it not be more poetic to say "alchemists", as in the medieval workshops?) prepare the pastes. But all this needs a guiding spirit, otherwise the work would lack intention and personality. The work of this factory is not anonymous, as might appear at first sight; each piece bears the indelible imprint of the craftsman, his most subtle "handwriting" characteristics. But above all is the style, which is a sum of qualities difficult to define: stylization, dynamism, colour, theme, quality of paste, etc. Each one separately and collectively reflects the spirit which created them. The Lladró brothers have found the unmistakeable definition of their work and every one of their collaborators are so imbued with their style that it emerges subconsciously from their work. First a piece is designed, within the limits of the style which characterizes every Lladró porcelain piece. Once the design has been agreed upon, the sculptor makes a clay model which is now ready to be analyzed from the points of view of its aesthetic, technical and commercial possibilities. The brothers themselves carry out this study on which will depend the future life of the piece. This is the moment when spirit and clay fuse to create a work of art. The three brothers put the piece to a secret vote and, if the result is unanimous, decide upon its final form: they study possible modifications, and its approximation to the firm's style and public tastes. It could be said that the future buyer of the piece is present —in spirit at

Divided into numerous and complicated parts, each one made in a special mould, Lladró porcelain figures are then recreated by delicate and expert hands, finally giving harmony to the finished work.

least— at this examination. Every piece is created to order, in the tradition of the most famous historical workshops, for example those of King-tö-chen, which worked according to the tastes of their European customers. Once every detail of the piece has been decided upon, a master model is made slightly larger than the definitive size to allow for shrinkage in the kiln. This master is then copied in plaster and remains as a fixed witness

to the whole creative process; its importance is so decisive that it must be subjected to a rigorous examination in which the most minimal details are treated by specialists who work with a delicate precision. Ways must now be studied to cut this figure up into different pieces so that it may be recreated later from moulds. This is one of the most delicate moments of the whole operation since the future harmony of the piece depends upon it: it is nothing less than the breaking up of the work which will lead to

its subsequent recreation. Each fragment of this complicated jigsaw must later fit with absolute precision if the model is to be perfectly recreated in every detail. Only the deepest knowledge of modelling techniques will ensure that the final result will have all the qualities and force of the finest sculptures. In this way the objects and figures created in the Lladró workshops offer not only a wide range of themes but

Careful finishing
touches and perfect
assemblies, following
the most ancient oriental
porcelainware
traditions, give
life, in successive
stages, to the original
model until it is
reconstructed in
every detail.

43

also an unequalled standard of modelling and finish.

While the specialists study the cutting up of the model and prepare the moulds, the paste is prepared in the laboratories of the Chemistry Department, according to formulae and preparations, the result of continual research and experimentation the fruits of which are zealously guarded. This somewhat dehumanised name denotes one of the most poetic and legendary aspects of porcelain manufacture.

The secrets of paste and raw materials were kept the closest of secrets and no outsider was allowed to penetrate the mysteries of this unattainable wisdom. The wise guardians of the secret in China were punished with death if ever they revealed it. Seventeenth-century European chemists have left us the most bizarre versions of what porcelain consisted of: "It is a certain mass composed of gypsum, oyster eggs, marine molluscs and other similar species", so one sage tells us, "which is formed into a mixture and then buried in a secret place. The head of the family reveals the secret to his sons only, and they leave the

An unsurpassed labour of investigation, a model for the most advanced porcelain industries, permits a constant development in the knowledge of pastes and colours and converts the increasingly difficult creative process into reality.

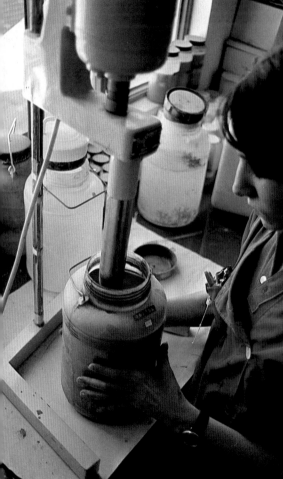

mixture under the ground for the space of eighty years, at which time they dig it up and make with it their exquisite transparent vessels''. Porcelain works, and specially the famous Chinese celadons, have been supposed to possess certain magic properties, among them the power to detect poisons by changing colour. Many kings used them as a defense against potential poisoners.

The paste, composed mainly of kaolin and water, is injected into a moistened mould and left to dry in a delicate process on which will depend the final quality of the figure.

Once a workable consistency has been reached the craftsmen set to the recomposition of the model.

Each one of the pieces from the different moulds is then polished manually by the hands of specialists.

Only in this way will the complete piece seem to have no joins and faithfully reproduce the original design conceived by the sculptor. Once all these rigorous and continual selection tests have been passed, then the piece has sufficient merit to bear the Lladró mark, guarantee of the work's quality, a cabalistic logotype linked to the most ancient traditions of alchemic symbols.

Every European porcelain maker has faithfully maintained this tradition, so appreciated by collectors who are constantly on the lookout for works signed by the major continental manufacturers. Ever since the

In the delicate manufacturing process the pieces have to be painstakingly perfected in order to reach the highest level of artistic quality. This is possible thanks to all those, like Rafael Badía, Cristóbal Calabuig, Salvador Castelló, Antonio García, Manuel Hurtado, Manuel Leonor, José Llisó, Dionisio Montañana, Vicente Navarro, José Miguel Piquer, Miguel Ramón, José Trujillo and so many other anonymous hands whose store of experience and high enthusiasm combine to achieve perfection.

first works appeared from the reputable workshops of Venice, Meissen, Vienna or Fürstenberg, the factory mark has been the stamp of guarantee offered to the buyer or collector to assure him of the perfect quality of each piece. The newly born work of art passes through a veritable baptism of fire in order to merit its paternity. This was not the case with the ancient Chinese porcelain industry since its works were largely anonymous with no mention of either factory or craftsman.

The moulds used to construct the figure and reproduce each one of its component parts are given a short lease of life to guarantee the perfection of the results. And at the merest sign of a defect the mould is destroyed and substituted with another which will give an absolutely faithful reproduction of the original model. In the case of special, numbered series all the moulds are destroyed once the quantity decided upon has been produced, every component being sacrificed in a ritual which is a fitting tribute to the most distinguished works of art. From this moment on the piece becomes unique and unrepeatable, available to a limited number of buyers only,

47

thus adding to its artistic value a justified mercantile value which results in the piece fetching enormous prices on the national and international markets, and becoming an authentic collectors' item. The pieces are now ready to be handed over to highly specialized painters, who ensure that the original colours are perfectly reproduced.

The reconstructed pieces are now ready to be painted. A specialized artist studies the colour creation on the original model and then carries out a test. The expert is familiar with not only the behaviour of the colours which will come into contact with high temperatures in the kiln, but also their aesthetic effect overall. His is a highly compromised task since he must decide one of the basic aspects in the evaluation of a piece of porcelain. Those works which acquire special prestige and high price do so largely on the basis of their colour, and the most famous porcelains are characterised artistically by the colour of their enamels. Thus we speak, for example, about the *green* porcelain of China, the *pink* family pertaining to the

Under the control of the decorators, each and every one of the figures receives the colour which then must be transformed by the action of fire. This genuine task of medieval miniaturists can only be carried out by people with solid experience and rigorous artistic training if the work is to reach the required level of perfection.

Yong-cheng epoch, or the *gentle enamels,* softer and thinner, which were used in the eighteenth-century oriental factories. Many ancient porcelain works of unquestionable aesthetic merit are less appreciated because of certain enamelling defects. European pastes needed a higher grade of firing than those used in China and, on hardening, did not allow the enamel to penetrate; for this reason today we find that *pictorial* relief in the decoration of many pieces of German or French porcelainware.

The composition of the kaolin paste has always been a decisive factor in order to determine the quality of porcelain. The Medicis were the first who managed to prepare homogeneous white pastes of a quality considerably superior to that of

50

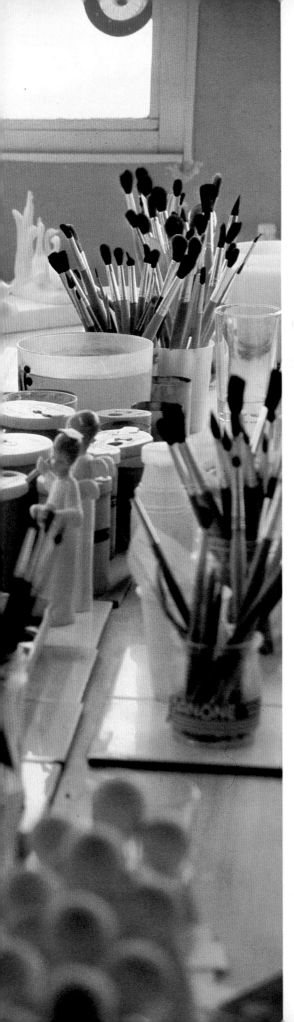

the porous pastes made in Europe at the time. But they guarded the secret so well that the discovery of this plastic material —which had the tendency to deteriorate considerably in the firing process— was lost with them.

The Chinese continued to be the sole possessors of the secret. They used for their porcelain a fire-resistant clay which was found in the hills near King-tö-chen: *kaolin*. This material, which turns white on firing, was discovered in Europe by a curious coincidence. In 1711 a German peasant had the incredible idea of dusting his wig with a certain white powder he had discovered in the Vale of Aue in Saxony. The servant of Böttger, an alchemist in the service of the Elector of

Saxony, used the same formula to powder his master's wig until the latter, surprised by the weight he was carrying on his head, examined and analyzed the supposed "flour", only to find that it was the famous and so long sought-after kaolin. Böttger's laboratory became a veritable strong box and his assistants were threatened with death if they revealed the "secret of the wigs". But the precaution had little effect: nine years later porcelain was being manufactured in Vienna.

In 1768 a French lady, the wife of a chemist, discovered in Saint-Yrieix a deposit of white earth which she thought would be a wonderful substance with which to make... soap! Her husband, M. Darnet, sent a sample to Sèvres where, from that moment on, some of the most artistic, valuable and delicate "soaps" in the whole of the history of art would be made with that earth.

The manufacture of porcelain no longer depends, thankfully, on these coincidences. The laboratories submit the different materials to rigorous examination, and analyze and experiment with colours and varnishes, until they achieve the tenuous chromatic range so characteristic of Lladró porcelain. But this scientific work is the fruit of years of experience and meticulous research which, due to its elaborateness, almost constitutes an "artistic secret" itself.

The painting and enamelling of the different pieces is a decisive moment in the creation of artistic porcelainware.

Expectant, like the delicate lady on the left, the figures are prepared to receive the materials which, once fired, will produce the glaze and brilliance, typical of porcelain. The sprinkling, which oriental craftsmen carried out with a perforated bamboo rod, must be totally even if the desired quality is to be achieved.

Highly experienced specialists carry out this delicate and wonderful task.

The pigments in their raw state do not correspond to their final colour, a circumstance which becomes more complicated if we bear in mind that there are more than five thousand different shades on the Lladró palette. In order to ease the painter's task, the pigments are stained with guide-colours. His task requires intense concentration and a steady wrist: a hand as tempered as those which the miniaturist painters of former times needed to paint their pictures in such minute detail.

When the figures have been given their exact tones and colours the moment has arrived to separate those pieces to be finished in matt from those which will have a shiny lustre.

The figures to be varnished receive the bluish shiny pigmentation characteristic of Lladró porcelain. The varnish is sprinkled over the figure, just as the celebrated oriental master craftsmen with their perforated bamboo rods used to do. It is a delicate operation since too thick a coating could spoil the plastic quality of the piece, while too thin a coating would cause the colours to lose their depth.

Porcelain is fundamentally a material of rich translucent tones. The varnish should contribute to this magic effect of light filtration which softens forms, enlivens the colour and increases the transparent quality of the material until it becomes a poetic substance.

On the other hand the matt pieces have been so conceived as a consequence of their aesthetic meaning; they are, like literary prose, a more straightforward and direct form of expression, charged with human content. Often the simplicity of a piece finished in matt accentuates the elementary elegance of porcelain. Shine is more spectacular; matt is more direct and its charm lies in the plasticity of the material itself. It is never

Throughout the manufacturing process numerous and rigorous quality controls select the works.
Plain or coloured pastes with or without glaze have to pass this test of perfection if they are to be awarded the magic Lladró logotype.

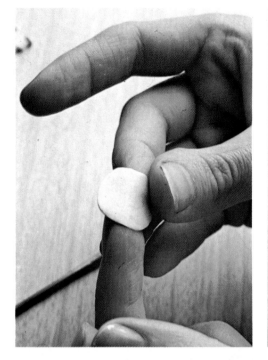

In the care of expert hands, flowers and other complements to porcelainware are made with absolute attention to detail. Petals, stamens, pistils and leaves are painstakingly modelled and put in place to produce those marvellous baskets which are the pride of Lladró porcelainware and patent examples of perfection nobly recognized by the most prestigious international firms.

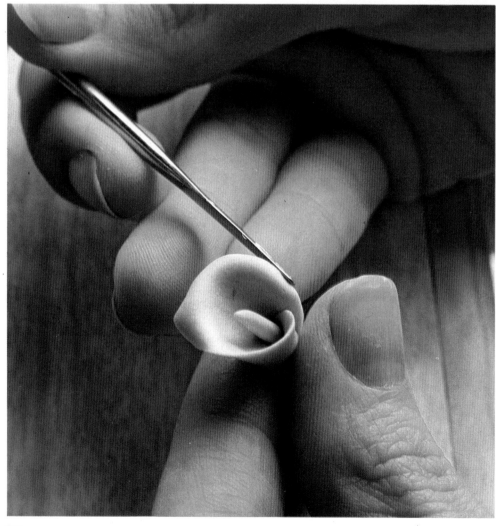

forgotten that the value of a piece of porcelain, like that of any special form, lies fundamentally in the inspiration of its shape and the delicacy of its design and composition. Very often simplicity is the result of a long process of artistic sedimentation, like those light, liquid brush strokes, apparently so effortless, with which Velázquez completed his paintings. It would seem that the artist were afraid to destroy, with excessive elaborateness, the natural magic of life.

This impressionistic vision does not exclude, on the other hand, meticulous application or very precise work. Many pieces require highly intricate finishing touches and their tiniest details must be treated almost microscopically. An infinite number of small elements —the handle of an umbrella or parasol, St Joseph's staff, a warrior's metal sword— must be

56

made separately and to do so requires an eyesight as fine as Dürer's.

All the intelligence and skill of the craftsmen is needed up until the very last stages in the making of a piece; in this way it becomes a unique product injected with the life of so many hearts and hands. As the years go by it will receive a new transfusion of life with the dedication of all those persons who will have loved, admired or possessed it.

These finishing touches are a showcase for the virtuosity of the craftsman; they are modelled by hand and created in a process of microscopic sensitivity. They are the details we can admire in the most complicated groups; the finish of a parasol, a flower petal, the band around a hat, all made with the warm direct touch of the artist. They are the final rounding-off to a work conceived as a synthesis of harmonies. A well made work comes into being by the same process that results in the virtuous life of the wise: through dedication and love, imagination and experience, applied to rude materials.

Many hours of work are needed to achieve these effects and details. But the value of a work of art transcends the effort that

The exquisite parasol carried by this beautiful lady is another of the difficult challenges overcome by the mastery of Lladró craftsmen. The most intricate laces and embroideries are faithfully reproduced with a microscopic precision which would satisfy even the most demanding clients.

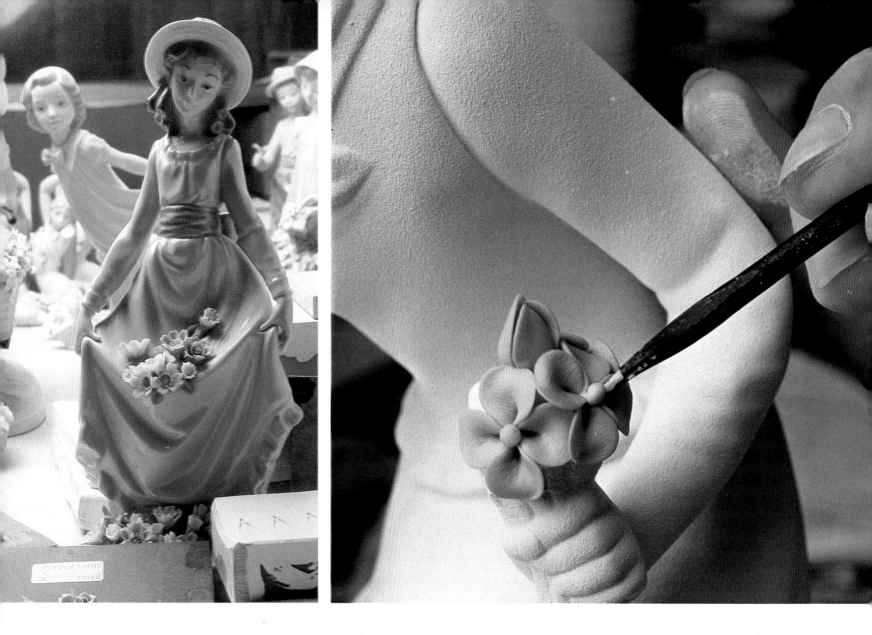

went to produce it. As Marcel Proust said, ''A work of art that displays the presumptuousness of endeavour is like a gift that still bears the price-tag''. For this reason the exquisite detail, achieved by dint of effort and dedication, should be incorporated into the group to enhance the beauty of the whole figure; if it is to stand out it must be modest and delicate, like the beauty of a woman or the virtue of the wise. It is no accident that the art of porcelainware originated in the Orient where the arts of .philosophy flourished. Could the

wisdom of Zen or the light of Buddha be better expressed than through the transparency of porcelain? Its whole process of creation is a search for perfect beauty in the smallest space and absolute simplicity of forms. The different pieces, once painted, varnished and finished, are ready to be fired. The kiln is like another artist in the team although it is somewhat unpredictable, a prey to sudden temper-tantrums. Has it not been said that a passionate temperament is made of fire? The kiln must be absolutely mastered if the work

is not to be ruined in this final stage of the operation. Hundreds of hours of delicate and patient work, precious seconds of creative inspiration, days of work and expectation can all be lost in an uncontrolled kiln. For this reason the specialists arrange the pieces according to the degree of heat they should receive. A few of them are fired in the old firewood or fuel oil kilns built by Vicente Lladró; the figures are forged in the fire; the heat reduces them to their final size and consolidates, harmonizes and synthesizes them,

60

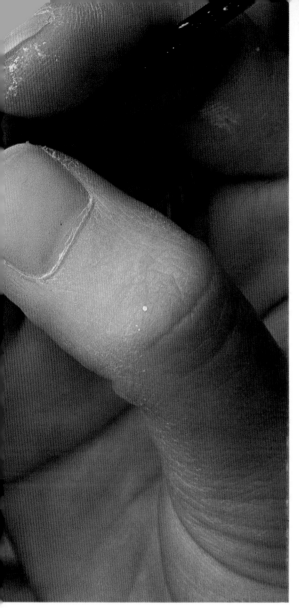

Once these complements have been made the steadiest of wrists is needed to put them in place or to fire them separately to be added at the last moment, depending on the technical demands of each piece. In brief, this type of work can only be carried out by great artists and craftsmen.

The moment of truth has arrived! Trial by fire is a reality here. This temperamental and unpredictable genius, the kiln, has to be tamed. The quality of the pastes or the colours, the correct arrangement of the pieces and the heat of the fire are not enough to permit the creation of these marvellous figures. It is also necessary to predict the reactions of the fire and the temperatures it produces, and to store up a massive reserve of experience and technical knowledge.

endowing them with exquisite plastic qualities. All that is needed now is a final touch and a painstaking quality control where pieces are subjected to a rigorous selection process.

These works will travel to the five continents where they will be the delight of sensitive people everywhere. They will outlive us, bearing our diminutive and humble message to future generations. They will be the secret witnesses of our daily life, our tastes and our sensitivity. The skyscrapers of Manhattan will speak of our technological conquests; but these small porcelain works will carry in their delicate and transparent skins the mark of a preoccupied and tormented civilization which held in its hands a gift of love.

Aesthetics and Themes in Lladró Porcelain

Customs and Everyday Life as a Basis for Expression

As an introduction to this fine book, it would be opportune to pinpoint some of the historical reasons why, still today, the more refined sectors of society feel a penchant for porcelain objects, in particular figurines or sculptured groups of small dimensions and fundamentally decorative in purpose.

In the first place, the attractiveness of small artistic creations is directly related, naturally enough, to the skill and imagination (and above all the ''good taste'') of the artists who model and paint them, although it is no less true that porcelain itself exercises an attraction through its own intrinsic qualities.

With the sporadic arrival of the first oriental porcelainware in Europe, artists struggled to imitate them, and before the discovery, in Meissen, of the first European kaolin porcelain, at the beginning of the eighteenth century, there were many chinaware imitations of those delicate pieces so much admired by society of the time. This creative enthusiasm coincided with a brilliant moment of the baroque period, in which the courts of kings and princes gave great importance to the decoration of banqueting tables. This pageantry was often completed with the guests' receiving coloured alabaster figures or woodcuts, either iconographic, popular or mythological in theme. Such figures could be considered the first antecedents to some of the ones which Lladró porcelain was to make world famous so many centuries later.

Since they first began to function, European manufactures were outstanding in their production of coloured porcelain figurines which represented burlesque themes or scenes from everyday life, made with great personality and decorativeness by artists such as Kändler and Bustelli, who established the real prototypes for porcelain figures during that century.

Fully aware of this valuable and rich past, the Lladró brothers have created an ample world of themes and characters, traditional or new to the field of decorative porcelain, but always bearing that highly characteristc stamp of their work.

Daily life, with its wealth of themes, has been a constant fountain of inspiration for creations in porcelain. The following pages offer a wide sample of this artistic trajectory.

The illustration shows one of the
most interesting pieces belonging
to the "elite" series which,
being of limited issue with each
piece numbered, has added
greatly to its market value.
The theme of this remarkable work
is a group of fishermen's fight
against the elements. The
dramatic effect has been achieved
through the intelligent use of
composition, particularly the
forced position of the boat, the
violent foreshortening of the
waves and the tension of each of
the protagonists. The group shows
an admirable knowledge of those
people who make their living from
the sea; observe the helmsman who
is the living image of the sea
dog, the oarsmen who display the
caution which is the fruit of
their long experience, and the
boy who, despite his years,
already instinctively respects
the maritime environment.

66

A difficult situation reveals the great skill of its creators: a group of fishermen wage a determined fight against a storm. This is one of the most outstanding group pieces to have been produced in porcelain. Groups require special dexterity since, simultaneously with the creation of each figure, every element within the composition has to harmonize with the whole. The problem has here been masterfully resolved and everything in the scene expresses action: the violent foreshortening of the boat, the forced postures of the fishermen, the expressive colour tones and the billowing waves all make their contribution. Other excellent elements are the strong character of the helmsman, the dramaticism of the boy in his desire to save his dog, and the vigilant tension of the two oarsmen.

The scene holds the spectator in suspense; the intense humanity of these figures struggling to save their lives makes us, as we contemplate the danger that lies in wait for them, long to see the waves calm once more, and in this way the artists achieve our

participation in the dramatic tension of the scene.

The application of colour presented serious difficulties in these cases. To achieve the dramatic effect strong colours which are of an unpredictable nature must be used; the kiln temperature always alters strong colours and these reactions must be very well known if the final result is to be the one desired. On the other hand a piece with these characteristics has to be made with different quality pastes for each different fragment —the oars, the waves and the boat, for example, each require a different technique, and must be made separately—, which means that the creative process becomes very slow since each piece has to be dried before the next one is tackled.

Staying with the maritime theme, and with similar difficulties to those of the previous piece, we find this bust of the brave helmsman. His tanned skin and the way in which he grabs the helm itself reveals a profound knowledge of the sea and its people. And this is hardly surprising since the lands of Valencia

The expressiveness of the
figures is the outstanding
characteristic of these three
details. The one on
the previous page shows the
strength of the oarsmen and the
terror of the dog caught amidst
the fury of the elements. On the
left we see the boat being tossed
about. Below we see
the determination of the straining
fisherman.

This piece, which offers us the severe image of the helmsman, is a homage to the men who live from the sea. The artist has understood and managed to express how those dedicated to a seafaring life become hardened by it.

Three excellent close-ups permit us to evaluate the piece in the way it deserves. Opposite we can admire the perfection of this manly face; above, a detail of the helm shows how the effect of wood eaten away by salt spray has been achieved. To the right: an excellent close-up of the young sailor's watchful tension.

have a long seafaring tradition to which the brothers have paid homage through the medium of clay: to the waters which bathe these coasts and the men who daily accept the sea's challenge.

Along with the storm scene, this group of card players in a tavern is one of the most interesting pieces to have been made in porcelain. Here we see four men immersed in a card game where bets play a fundamental role. The scene is set in the eighteenth century and the artists have created a complicated style which perfectly reflects the idea we all have of the card-sharp. We are in that epoch (so magnificently described by Dumas in *The Three Musketeers*) which abounded in street and tavern brawls. Here there are two musketeers in the contest; both their expressions are tense and their bodies are poised for action at the slightest provocation. While the player on the left thinks over his move the other impatiently tells him to play his hand without more ado. A third figure, who could easily be the tavern keeper, watches the proceedings alertly, while a fourth observes the game with cold interest.

This study is the result of a combination of several pieces. Only the floor, with the barrel and the dog,

was made as a single unit; every other element had to be made separately and then added to the whole. Great attention has been paid here to detail —the pack of cards, for example, is based on similar packs from contemporary engravings— which required profound research so that no element would clash with the overall atmosphere, and so that this concern for detail would be a major facet of the porcelainware under examination here.

The artist captures out attention through the atmosphere created by the composition of the piece. Close examination reveals a subtle interplay between forces and stylized forms. The two seated players constitute lateral forces which are compensated for by the vertical force of the standing musketeer. The figures have been stylized to ensure that the compensatory interplay of tensions in the composition would be elastic and free of violence. There is a very definite dynamism at work here, not of actual movement but of a sense of expectation at a possible action in the near future, the threatened unleashing of pent-up tensions.

It could be said that porcelain possesses ideal qualities for the recreation of the feminine world:

The Landau *is one of the pieces which best evokes the tranquility of nineteenth-century life. The artist's intention here has been to recreate that period in order to express the serenity of young ladies, from rich families, who used to ride in landaus. The main difficulty of the piece was to disguise the support points, but the problem has been perfectly resolved.*

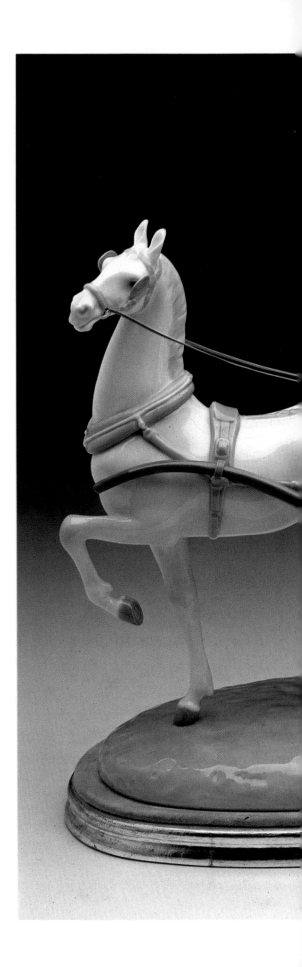

that universe full of simplicity and the chores of daily life. Such is the case with a series of studies from which we have selected those we consider most representative. The innocence and delicacy evoked by these works correspond to the artist's predilection for these scenes from last century. They are studies full of life in which the technical difficulties in their realization struggle against the exigencies of detail which the artist has imposed upon himself. The parasol belonging to the girl bending forward faithfully reproduces the texture of the tulle from which they are made, a remarkable feat of virtuosity on the part of its creator.

The horse's majestic gait, the elegance of the coachman and the graceful lines of the landau in this study endow it with that dignified and relaxed air we associate with educated young girls of the last century. The refinement which characterized the epoch allows the artist to marry the nineteenth-century environment to the delicacy of porcelain. This was the century which saw the both the birth and the splendour of romanticism, evoked by the piece illustrated.

The range of shades varies the distances which separate pink from red, and permits the different intensities of blue and the infinite varieties of grey. The whole piece is based on these colours, and their admirable blends are yet another demonstration of the artist's skill. The problem of the fragility of porcelain has been masterfully resolved: the points of support essential for the piece are intelligently placed and, camouflaged with considerable cleverness, pass unnoticed by the carefree young passengers.

For those who genuinely appreciate porcelain, and for the art lover or collector, this piece has an added valve since it is one of the most sought after limited series. The same is true of the piece entitled *Family Rally.* This is one of the pieces where every element has been treated in minute detail —the

This piece, called Family Rally, *is one of the best examples of the use of anecdote as the theme for a porcelain work. The different elements combine to offer us a scene in which activity holds the stage: the gentleman holds on to his Derby hat, the little girls jump about in their curiosity and the chauffeur kicks at a stray dog.*

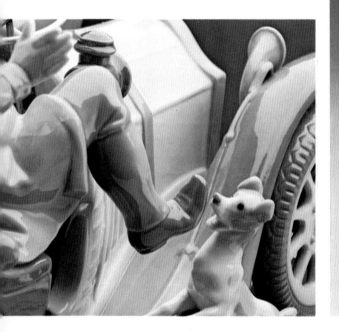

speedometer, for example. In this vision of daily life we return to the world of complex groups. The novelty of the automobile when it first appeared is marvellously captured here: a chauffeur takes a family for their first ride in the new machine. Anecdote is the undoubted protagonist of the scene: our eyes discover the bewilderment of the mother whose husband calms her fears, catch the chauffeur taking a kick at a stray dog, and delight in the little girls' curiosity at everything they see.

The family's excitement at such a novelty is offset by the delicate colouration of the piece: the three colours used —light brown, blue and grey— confer upon the group a necessary feeling of harmony.

One might wonder why the piece was not set in the present; but this would have caused a problem: the

The different perspectives which these illustrations offer permit us to observe the attention to detail on this piece; the perfection of the clothes, the dashboard with its speedometer, rev-counter, etc., are excellent samples of the care which went into their modelling.

*The stable scene is an idealized
vision of country life, seen from
the point of view of city people
who long for the repose which the
country offers.*

*The little girl with kittens is
one of a multitude of everyday
subjects given life through
porcelain. This particular piece
is enlivened by the mother cat's
attempt to clamber up the girl's
skirt to see her offspring.*

difficulty of blending together the delicacy of
porcelain and modern industrial technology.
Consequently the solution was to seek out an epoch
when the automobile was a sophisticated and by no
means common machine. By placing the theme at the
turn of the century the author was able to evoke
that romantic world of *Genevieve*.

This nostalgic vision of the past can thus take its
place beside all the scenes which evoke the thousand
details of everyday life, like that of the young girl
leaning upon her cow. It has a totally rustic air; the
girl has just milked the animal and now she stops to
watch the calf sniffing at the recently drawn and still
warm liquid. Her expression reveals her satisfaction
at the efficiency with which she has carried out the
work, while the peace of labours completed endows
her figure with that serenity so characteristic of
feminine tasks.

The piece has been made with admirable
mastery: the arms resting on the animal's great back,
the girl's tired expression and the gentleness of the
cow, the attitude of the calf and the placing of the
pail all reveal the skilful interplay of perspectives,
combining different sizes and exploiting the gaps
created in the scene to enhance the relief of the
composition.

The simple concept of the girl with the cow and
calf is similarly evident in other small figures which
follow the models established by the most accredited
European workshops of the eighteenth and nineteenth
centuries, recreated now by the Lladró sculptors.
Among these is the study of a little girl carrying some

The figures of the sailor and the young Dutch milkman reveal the extreme care which went into the tiniest details of costume and infant personality. The close-up gives us a better idea of the delicate modelling of the hand and the admirable way in which the resistance of the ceramic material was overcome. On this page is another little boy pushing a barrow full of an immense variety of flowers. The most interesting aspect of this piece is the decorativeness of the colourful flowers.

delightful kittens in her lap. The scene is completed by the presence of the kittens' mother who tries to climb up her skirt. The bluish tones and the gentleness of the forms accentuate the delicacy with which the theme has been treated. The innocence of the little girl as she marvels at these tiny beings she is carrying in her apron is wonderfully displayed in her expression and gesture. One might say that all these figures transmit to us the delicate messages of the infantile soul.

Within these limits of artistic concern, and similar in theme, are the studies of two little boys, one dressed as a Dutch milkman carrying two pails and the other as a sailor with a boat in his hands, in which special attention has been paid to facial expression and delicacy of posture. The interplay of gentle shades is based solely on three colours, cream, blue and brown, deliberately limited in order to enhance the perfection of the modelling technique.

Other figures can be taken as models of perfection, such as the little boy pushing a barrow full of flowers. This is one of the most colourful and lively pieces. The flowers capture our attention and themselves constitute a delicate work of art. The chromatic contrast of their petals, and the delicacy of form, especially visible in the rosebuds which are on the point of opening, create a remarkably decorative effect. The same could be said of the young milkman, whose hands hold two full pails.

The piece which depicts a young girl with a jar is a superb illustration of the renaissance poetic and musical tradition. Delicious madrigals speak to us of young peasant girls gathered around a fountain and living the most varied experiences; songs such as *Prado Verde y Florida* (Green Flowery Meadow) and *En la Fuente del Rosel* (At the Fountain of the Rosebush). These renaissance scenes evoke that world of poetry inspired by nature and peasant men and women. Porcelain could hardly resist the temptation to develop these themes as neither could stoneware, the material from which the piece illustrated was made.

The young jar-carrier pulls up in front of her curious onlookers watching her at her work and adopts a very feminine pose: while holding the jar nimbly in one hand she puts the other on her hip and, with perfect ease of manner, asks us, "What are *you* staring at?". She then carries on with her task totally

The harmony of the composition can be appreciated in this detail. Two volumes confer a necessary balance upon the whole: the backward inclined body of the young girl and the pitcher, which compensates for this.

The possibilities of stoneware
have been exploited in the figure
of the girl with pitcher.
The beauty of the peasant girl
is offset by the position of
her limbs. The colours are those
which the earth offers naturally.

unconcerned and in total innocence.

Lladró porcelain rejoices in a large number of small figures which depict simple scenes from everyday life. Its divers subject matter includes scenes which we would hardly relate to other creations but which are here revealed with a new spirit. They are subjects which were abreadly exploited in the arts of ancient Greece and Rome; juvenile delicacy and charm used as a subterfuge to awaken in the observer sentiments of love, tenderness and respect for ordinary lives which palpitate everywhere and at all times.

This young girl watering her flowers is the perfect opportunity for the artist to join two worlds, infancy and flora, in one single piece. Both have the common denominator of freshness of form.

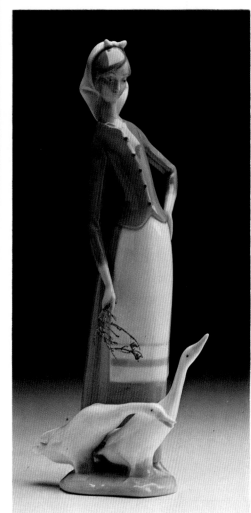

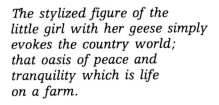

The stylized figure of the little girl with her geese simply evokes the country world; that oasis of peace and tranquility which is life on a farm.

One puppy sniffs at the little girl's toe in the happy expectancy of being possibly the first to receive some honey. Anecdote has been ingeniously captured here.

Good examples of this special vision of the world of everyday things are implicit in the figure of a little girl guilelessly watering her roses or the stylized study of a young girl, with a twig in her hand, taking a pair of geese for a walk. A group of delightful Dalmation puppies look on fixedly while their little mistress puts her finger into a jar of honey: they know she will let them have a taste. One of the puppies sniffs at her toes in anticipation of the treat in store, though he is not sure which is the right toe to sniff! In another scene below we see a pair of goats around a young girl who holds and caresses a little

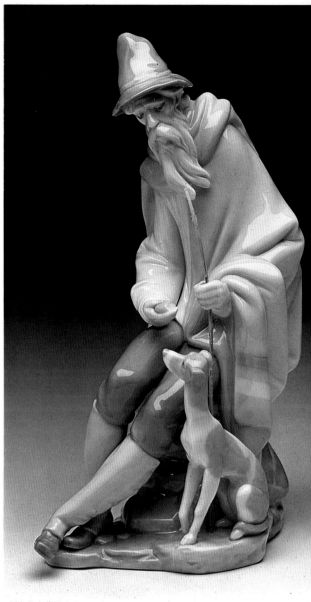

The bond between man and his faithful companion from the animal kingdom can be seen in this piece depicting a beggar with a stray dog.

The tenderness with which this girl caresses the little kid seems to suggest feminine understanding of the mystery of maternity.

Here the author has chosen a scene which illustrates the ingenuousness of the infant world: a little girl puts her hand to her head in consternation at having dropped her basket of flowers.

This young girl leaning on her basket expresses an attitude of dreamy abandon characteristic of this age of woman.

An amusing little redhead, with her hair tied in two pretty pigtails, evokes the love which all children feel for animals.

The carefree nature of young children is expressed here by this girl who abandons her jar to stroke a puppy.

Next page: the exquisite poem by Juan Ramón Jiménez, Platero y Yo, has been freely interpreted in this study.

kid. Both the happy gesture of the little girl giving honey to her puppies and the serene face of the blind man advanced in years have been captured excellently. The old man's grey beard help to confer upon him that repose and dignity of old age, while the stylization of dog and master gives them both an air of great elegance.

Four little girls invite us into their world of innocence. Though each one displays a different attitude the four together have one common denominator: the delightful impression which the simplest scenes produce in us. One girl rests her head on her left arm and sits beside her basket of lettuces, her mind wandering among the clouds of some romantic idea. Another puts her hand to her head in consternation: she has dropped her basket of flowers. Another girl blissfully cuddles a little lamb, her mind on nothing else.

This delightful series of children with animals would have been incomplete without the little boy and his donkey. The joy with which the boy hugs the animal takes us inside the famous poem by Juan Ramón Jiménez, *Platero y Yo.* This scene is a free interpretation of the poet's text, and the delicate form of the animal is extraordinarily suited to porcelain. The little boy, dressed as a Mexican, nuzzles the coat of the animal with his cheek, while contentment radiates from his face. The donkey stands in a comic posture and his merry eyes appear to display as much happiness as the little boy.

Mention has already been made of the world of flowers, one of the marvels of Lladró porcelain. The arduous work which went in to their modelling is overshadowed by the refinement with which they have been painted and arranged. On contemplating the floral pieces one would almost swear they possess

The illustrations on this page offer two new examples of one of the favourite themes for porcelain: a little girl with flowers. In both cases the flowers are the predominant element and centre of attraction. The close-ups allow us to appreciate the attention to detail.

the real properties of subtle vegetable material. Good examples of this are scenes such as the one where one girl waters her roses with a watering-can while another marvels at her own flowers. The close-ups allow us to see in detail the remarkable way in which the roses and tulips of each girl respectively have been made, painted and arranged.

In another scene a sleeping dog lets himself be pampered by his mistress, a young shepherd-lass who, seated on the floor, rests her head on her friend's shoulder. The shepherd-boy has removed his hat so that it will not disturb his companion and the tenderness of his expression and his protective stance, lightly suggested, give a special quality to the study.

By the side of the children resting with their dog we find another couple of little shepherds: she in typical peasant costume and he wearing a cape. The little girl looks at her hands in a characteristically flirtatious way while he, surprised, watches the gesture over her shoulder.

The collections of small figures which, in fact, are different studies of the same person, are especially

The harmonious composition of this study of two little peasant children shows the little girl observing her hands in a flirtatious way, while the little boy curiosity watches this gesture he has yet to understand.

The creator of this piece took absolute care in chosing a subject which would best reflect the innocence of children. The pleasant facial expressions harmonize with the dog's placid sleep.

The illustrations on this page
offer us two series of pieces
dealing with two different themes.
The upper porcelain
study shows a young
girl trying out different
postures with her straw boater,
while the one on the left of
this text reveals four little
girls in nightshirts in various
positions. The young girl with
boater is also a study in colour
combinations: the six pastel
shades of the dress and the other
six tones of the belt. It is not
difficult to appreciate here the
virtuosity of the creator and his
degree of maturity as an artist.

The dance has provided subject matter for innumerable works of art, above all in painting and sculpture. Porcelain is also a highly suitable medium through which to express such a suggestive theme, and the four ballerinas below are a marvellous example. The artist has demonstrated his knowledge of the elasticity of dancers' bodies, here depicted in four different postures.

This group of six little girls coquettishly making up at a dressing table is an exquisite study of ease of manner.

The elasticity of dancers' bodies has been captured here through stylization of form and lightness of posture. The close-up of the young girl's face expresses the sweet charm of a nascent idyll. Left: the little girl with her cat once again takes us back to the world of innocence, depicted through the coexistence between children and animals.

This scene, depicting a young girl with an umbrella and geese, has been captured in such a way as to raise it up to the level of artistic theme.

Right: the amusing fight between a goose and a dog is offset by the surprise on the little peasant girl's face.

interesting. They are veritable studies in colour, form and posture and are evidence of a creativity which, far from heading towards extinction, is in the fullness of its powers and constantly on the lookout for new forms of expression. Such is the case of the group of six girls who, showing off coquettishly, comb their hair and adorn themselves as if they were seated at a dressing table. The groups of the four little boys in nightshirts and the six girls sporting hats in every ·manner possible are both authentic studies in each theme. Similarly the four ballerinas who appear in a great diversity of postures on the two previous pages constitute a highly characteristic study of this subject. All these repetitions of the same figure at different moments attempt collectively to capture, as a film sequence might do, the different aspects of a person's psychology.

In other cases the artist joins different elements with their own individual personality in a single piece; an illustration of this is the scene featuring a couple of dancers. He is sitting on the floor, she on a seat, and as their gazes intertwine and their bodies relax from the dance an idyll is born. The dance has traditionally been one of the most attractive themes for creators of works of art. Painters have used the subject since earliest times and yet it was not until Degas that this age-long theme —here one remembers the ballerinas which the Egyptians painted on their murals— found its most celebrated exponent. Porcelain, for its part, is a most natural medium with which to capture the gentle harmony of bodies moving in time to music. In the case of the piece in question, this has been underlined by the stylization of the figures of both dancers. On the other hand it is worth noting the novel treatment of the musculature of the bodies here; his neck, arms and

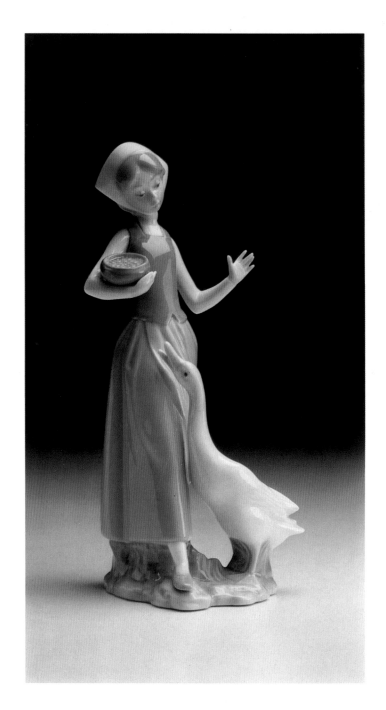

legs and her collar bone have been modelled in such a way as to faithfully reproduce the forms of bodies which enjoy constant exercise.

The combination of blues and greys which colour the young girl who, umbrella in hand, goes for a walk accompanied by a flock of geese, serves to give unity and equilibrium to the piece; the golden colour of the umbrella handle adds a touch of contrast to this two-tone range, and the composition is balanced by the open umbrella and the geese which waddle at the girl's feet.

The scene where a goose gaggles indignantly at its inability to jump from its basket to face the barking dog below is wonderfully anecdotal and stylized and offers a well distributed range of colours: greys, blues and browns.

The situations of daily life are innumerable. The scenes with shepherds, hunters, children and animals, dancers, flowers, etc., constitute an extensive gallery given form in porcelain. It could even be said that this is the favourite theme by virtue of its suitability to porcelain's plasticity. The legacies of the Orient and romanticism are evident here.

The nineteenth century brought to Europe a movement which widely advocated a return to Nature and the simple life: romanticism. Its central idea was to raise the 'mundane' to the level of art. Literature and painting rejoiced in intimate scenes of peasant life, just as the pieces we can admire in these illustrations do. Their creators have intelligently exploited the legacy of Europe's past, incorporating both oriental and romantic tendencies in their work but detatching them from their original meaning. Their work has a simple objective: to bring the wider public closer to an art which was traditionally reserved for the ruling classes. That their objective has been fulfilled is proven by the fact that Lladró pieces, considered to be among the most popular in the world, today decorate thousands of homes.

94

Following page: a shepherd boy watches intently over his flock, while the illustration above right depicts the charming scene of a young Eskimo boy playing with a white bear cub. Below, a young girl watches her herd of little pigs.

The enormous popularity of these works derives from the simplicity of their themes and the good taste with which they have been given form. A good example of this is the young shepherdess who tries to repel a goose which impatiently attempts to eat from the plate of food she is carrying.

Another magnificent figure is that of the shepherd who, seated on a pile of stones, alertly watches over his flock. At the same time a ewe contemplates her lamb's attempts to rise from the

This gallery of everyday scenes would have been incomplete without studies of traditional costume from a variety of different places. Right: a beautiful little girl marvellously attired carries a bouquet of flowers as an offering to the Virgin. Above: close-up of the girl's face showing the delicacy of her infant's features. Above right: porcelain study of a girl in Valencian costume bringing an offering highly characteristic of her land: a basket of oranges. Below right: another little girl repels a goose which is pecking at her dress.

ground. The artist's skill can be observed above all in the naturalness of the shepherd's hands.

The figure of a little Eskimo playing with a charming white bear cub is especially decorative by virtue of the acute way in which the artist has exploited the colour of his clothing. The boy's soft cap and the little bear are the definite centres of attraction of the whole piece.

Mention has already been made of the young girl with her herd of piglets. The girl gives off an air of simplicity perfectly in keeping with her rested posture.

A chapter with its own personality, and which could not have been overlooked, is that of the rich folklore of Valencia. The pieces selected are

wonderful examples: two young girls sporting traditional costume and bringing offerings to the Virgin. One carries luscious oranges —the most apt symbol of the Valencian *huerta*— while the other brings a lovely bouquet of carnations, yet another instance in which the makers of this porcelainware have faced the greatest modelling difficulties.

The delicacy of porcelain is revealed in an exemplary way in the figure representing a girl gathering flowers with which to make a bouquet. Two elements here catch the eye immediately: the girl's graceful posture and the fragility of the flowers she is picking.

Another little girl sports typical costume and headgear and carries a bunch of flowers in her left

Three enchanting little girls appear on this page. In the first place we see a delicate little creature gathering flowers; above: another girl in traditional Valencian costume holds a bunch of carnations. The third illustration shows a girl with goose and goslings.

hand. The figure was made in stoneware and its modelling is perfection itself.

We see similar spontaneity in the figure of a little girl who with one hand attempts to shoo away a goose which is pecking at her dress, while in the other she carries a basket of eggs snatched away from the indignant bird. To the right we see another girl sitting among a goose and her goslings.

The possibilities of stoneware are admirably exploited in the figure of a pair of children protecting their dog from the terrible wind. Blended whites, reds

This page: the composition above is a masterful study of cold and wind, in which two children protect their little dog from the inclemency of the weather. Above right we see the beautiful piece depicting a little girl dropping her flowers. The close-up immediately below it shows the delicacy of her hands.

and ochres are ideal colours for the material used. Along with the theme itself the clothes constitute a fundamental aspect of the piece. The little boy wears thick woollen socks held up by the laces of his rope sandals, a brilliant red cap and an ochre-coloured tunic to protect him from the constant bitter wind. The girl sports a dress the colour of her companion's cap and covers herself with a thick woollen shawl. We almost feel the cold ourselves as we observe the way in which she wears the shawl wrapped up to her nose and hugs the puppy, while he covers her body with his own. The timid expression on the little dog's face is also a response to the rigorous weather. In the composition of the piece the artist took into account the solid way in which the protagonists had to stand in order not to be bowled over, but any sensation of heaviness has been eliminated by the dynamic treatment of the theme. The famous expression 'inclement weather' here carries all its

weight, marvellously embodied in the defenselessness of these three feeble creatures.

The figure of the girl who has dropped her flowers is as decorative as the previous piece is tense. She is all colour: her hair is reddish, her blouse is bluish-green, her apron is striped in red, her hat is white, her dress is yellowish-ochre and the flowers stand out palely against the green leaves. The four principal colours —red, ochre, green and white— merge together to give the piece its characteristic harmony and gentle shades. Its theme resides simultaneously in two aspects: anecdote (the falling flowers) and the girl's comic posture. Her slightly bent knees and her outstretched arms both form part of her attempt to prevent the flowers and her hat falling at the same time. Once again the dynamics of the piece constitute the anecdote itself, elevating it to the category of theme.

Two little girls appear as variations on the same

This little girl in her sumptuous clothes is a study in profound timidity. Her sweet features are half hidden because she looks downwards in embarrassment at our admiring

gaze. The artist has captured perfectly that characteristic habit children have of putting their hands behind their back when they feel self-conscious, or uncomfortable.

theme: the guileless timidity of infancy. Both belong to the stoneware series dedicated to children. The first study depicts a little girl with her eyes lowered and her hands behind her back. This little peasant girl with her long tresses is coyly aware of us gazing at her magnificent dress. The long voluminous skirt is complemented by a delightful hat and a pair of clogs which make her tiny form slightly taller. She is in fact dressed like an adult and it is this which is the cause of her shyness and embarrassment. Her little face enhances the guilelessness of her personality: her snub nose, her pressed-in lips and her downward-looking eyes hiding from view.

Another endearing facet of feminine psychology has been captured in these two figures representing two little girls who, playing with their dolls, prelude the delights of maternity.

On the following page we see the piece representing a little girl with her pot of flowers. The smooth childlike forms of her face can be admired in the detail above while in the one below we can appreciate the texture of the hand.

The young peasant girl, bustling about in search of water with which to water the pot of flowers she carries in her left arm, is the subject of a fundamentally decorative piece which uses colour and anecdote to attract attention. The colours range widely from the white of the kerchief and the apron to the blue of the dress, through the yellow of the blouse, the rust-colour of the flower pot and the green and pink of the plant. The girl looks in wonderment at the plant, which grows daily in size and beauty thanks to her loving care.

"The face is the mirror of the soul"; so goes the old Spanish proverb which time has confirmed over and over again. There are exceptions, of course, but these simply confirm the rule. Since the dawn of time the artist has made portraits —faithfully, idealistically or imaginatively— that reflect the personality of the real or imaginary object of his love.

Two types of portrait have been cultivated through the centuries: formal and psychological. Formal portraits attempt solely to capture the likeness of the subject, while the latter type tries to reveal the personality of the subject through facial expression. Glorious examples of the first type are the faces of the *Greek Poseidon*, Michaelangelo's *David* and the *Venus de Milo;* while maximum achievements of the

second type are Goya's *Family of Charles IV,* or Rodin's *Balzac.* Naturally those portraits whose purpose is not to reveal psychology have to be idealized or invented, since those of live subjects cannot avoid revealing certain personality traits, however small.

Porcelain is a material of subtle characteristics which make it an ideal medium with which to express the smoothness and gentleness of the feminine face, as we can see in these two almost life-size studies of a girl's head. In reality we see only the face since the head is covered with a simple kerchief of cloth which the kiln has transformed into porcelain.

This is an imaginary portrait of a young girl meant to express a personal vision of beauty and purity. Her forehead is almost completely obscured by a crudish fringe of blond hair. Her eyes have a subtly intelligent look full of inner richness, and are perfectly framed by the gentle curve of the eyebrows. Her nose, like those of the happy and lively little girls in previous pieces, is small and snub. Her well-formed lips bear the full, rich pink colour of youth, while the chin and cheeks are lightly suggested in order not to detract from the other features. There is nothing about this face suggestive of firmness; quite the contrary: it is all gentleness and a prototype of

feminine beauty as seen by the artist. This work has become a veritable novelty in the world of porcelain by virtue of the originality of its theme.

The idealized beauty of that girl's face becomes converted, in the Eskimo figurines, into a vehicle to reflect the ideals of the infantile world. Here we return to the magic world of children to find it interpreted in a new way: the archetypal image of 'child' in a hostile Polar environment which, nevertheless, is powerless to steal from these children their characteristic charm, delicacy and ingenuousness. An example of this is a pair of little Eskimos sleeping soundly despite their

uncomfortable positions. The girl is wrapped in a blanket up to her nose with a lock of her long straight hair lying on top. The little boy rests his head on his arms folded over his legs which, in both cases, are drawn in as the only means to retain body heat.

The clothes are realistically coloured: their purely utilitarian purpose, that of giving warmth, does not allow for lavish and vivid decoration. The coarse texture of the fabrics is perfectly reproduced here in porcelain, which has been worked with supreme skill in order to give it the appearance and feel of stoneware. These two pieces together constitute a unique pair with highly individual characteristics,

Below: this pair of little Eskimos expresses admirably the recuperative power of children's sleep.

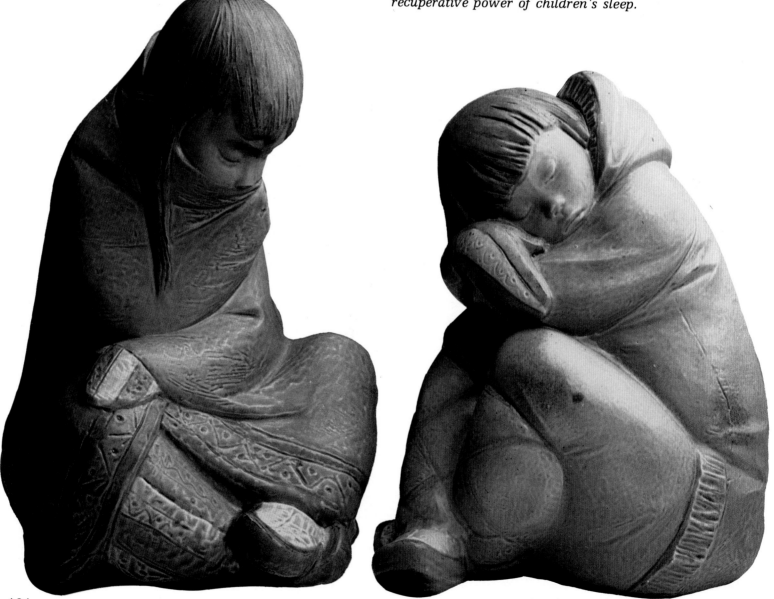

Another pair of Arctic children, on this page, represents one of the most successful achievments of infantile expression: the little girl is overcome with fatigue, while the little boy is full of hope.

while serving a practical purpose since they are, in fact, bookends. Despite the texture similar to stoneware, the children's faces are characteristically smooth by virtue of the mastery with which the material has been worked: the girl sleeps soundly while the boy's expression expresses the impassiveness of deep slumber.

Staying with the theme of Eskimo children, now given form in stoneware pieces, we find another study in which a little girl shows signs of fatigue —she bends at the knees and her eyes are closed— while a little boy, who could easily be her brother, holds her comfortingly to prevent her falling.

The clothes are slightly more colourful on this occasion. There are coloured trimmings on the sleeves and top of the boy's coat and on the edging of his hide boots. Nevertheless the rigours of the climate still

dominate, permitting no more elaborate decoration. Overlooking for a moment the white and blue of the trimmings, the range of colour is limited to different shades of brown, and this chromatic unity adds greatly to the harmony of the piece.

The little girl's defenseless air can be included perfectly in that ingenuous and gentle spirit of femininity which appears again and again throughout this extensive series of pieces. Her half-closed eyes and slightly sagging lips are signs of her fatigue while, on the other hand, the penetrating gaze of her brother suggests that there is still hope that their exhaustion will find deserved relief in a prolonged rest.

The same repose, which the two Eskimo children long for, positively emanates from the young girl sewing with absolute concentration, unaware of being observed. She is a typical Majorcan seamstress as her carefully and accurately modelled costume shows. Special care has also been taken in the making of the chair, the fretwork back of which was achieved by painstakingly cutting out fragments of paste to give the impression of work in wood.

105

An intimate understanding of the feminine soul and character shows through this study of a typical Majorcan embroiderer, on the left. Special care has been taken to reproduce the costume of these island women whose main occupation is tambour embroidery.

The little boy fishing, who appears above left on the following page, is a combination between the placidness of infancy and the coarseness of the sport of fishing. The illustration above right on the same page is a lively image of childhood: two little companions playing on a see-saw and watched by their somewhat bewildered dog.

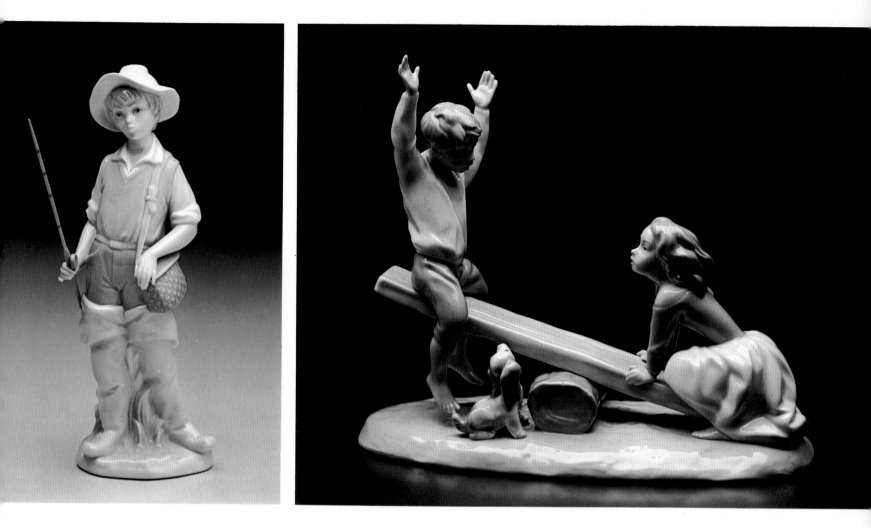

This piece is a unique portrayal of the feminine spirit: the tranquility of the scene and the delicacy of the girl's features combine to form an image of serenity. Note particularly the frailty of the hand holding the needle and her totally unruffled expression.

Her costume is worthy of special attention. The kerchief covering her head and the fine apron complement her skirt and blouse, richly decorated with borders and floral motifs in tenuous and varied colours. The characteristics of porcelain itself also give the colours a special quality which completes the harmony of the group. Though deliberately elegant, and refined, this piece nevertheless communicates to us the natural simplicity of the young embroiderer.

Certain characteristics should be emphasized here, in particular the colour of the hands and face of the young woman, on one side, and, on the other, the vision of peace, tinged with nostalgia, which placid provincial life reflects.

The simplicity of the feminine world gives place, once again, to the innocent world of children in two highly representative pieces. One is a fishing scene and the other shows children playing their interminable games. On this occasion two scenes from daily life have been chosen and, though on the surface they appear to have nothing in common, they share the theme of children's eagerness to know everything. This intense curiosity is perfectly reflected in the face of the little girl who has just given her playmate a strong push on the makeshift see-saw. The dog observes the scene obviously surprised, though not to the same extent as the little boy who suddenly finds himself in mid-air!

The serene vocation of this pair of singing nuns, which we can appreciate in the illustrations on this double page, has been sublimated by the delicacy of hands and fingernails, and the winged caps.

If the previous scene is an illustration of children's energy, the one depicting a boy fishing has chosen another path. The idea here was to take a fundamentally unpoetic theme, fishing, and endow it with the innocence and gentleness of the infantile world: the 'fisherman' is not a man; he is a child.

Earlier it was said that the creators of this porcelainware were conscious of the fact that the universe of small daily tasks and the world of women are inseparably joined. These concepts are prefectly expressed by the scene which depicts two nuns singing from a score in an atmosphere of complete intimacy and naturalness. Thanks to this piece we are able to glimpse the solitude of these sisters in religion and momentarily to share this intimate world without our intrusion being noticed.

The composition of the piece lays special emphasis upon the nuns' starched headgear and the score, both of which in some way symbolize their

detatchment from the world outside. The seclusion of this serenely harmonic environment is reflected in the attitude of the sister who sings and in the concentration of her listening companion.

If we look closely at these sisters' headgear we become aware of the enormous technical skill which went into their modelling. The slight curve in the form was necessary to prevent the weight of the paste itself from causing the caps to collapse during firing. The excellent detail of the faces permits us to appreciate the perfection of these nuns' features which reflect the purity of their lives and their dedication to daily tasks.

The maturity with which the previous piece was modelled gives way to the total mastery displayed by the figure representing a reclining girl who watches a little bird which has landed by her side. This peasant girl's face is a picture of calm, tenderness and interest in the tiny creature which has interrupted

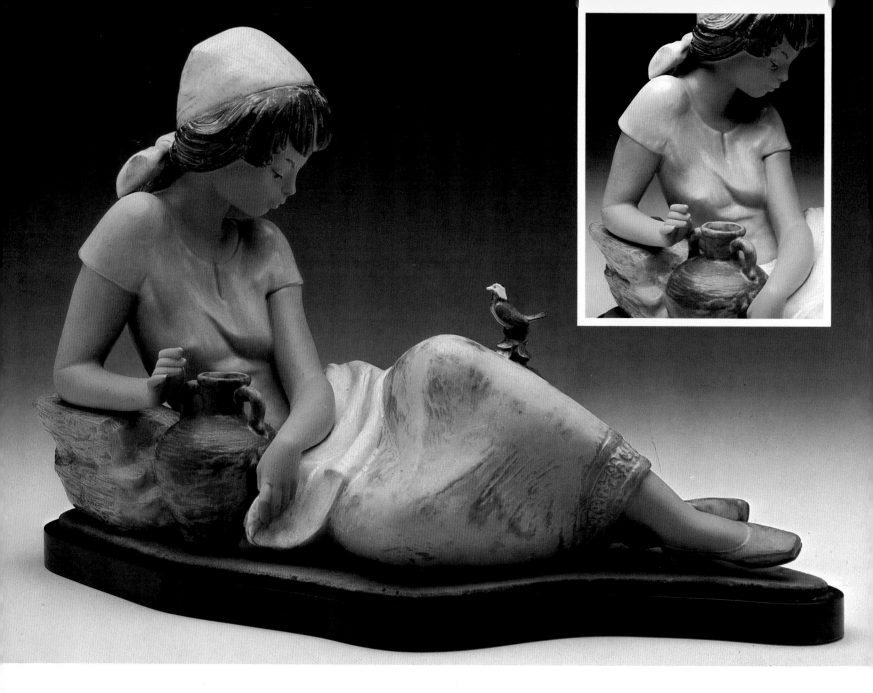

her repose; only her hand, slightly apart from the jar, gives away her mild surprise.

Here we find a most interesting characteristic: the mark left by the artist's hand can be clearly seen in the flutes of the young peasant girl's dress. This was invisible in the initial stages, but the firing process brought the imprint to light. The allegory which, to a certain extent, the piece embodies responds to that principle by which feminine detail and intimacy are so suitable for modelling into small works.

Above: The beautiful and interesting example of a stonework piece. A gentle counterpoint is established between the innocence of the young girl and the inoffensiveness of the bird; one could say that the artist's intention has been to pay homage to the purity of adolescence. The graceful outline of the youthful body is heightened by the care which went into the treatment of composition and colour.

Dynamism: a Centuries-old Desire

Ever since man first felt the creative urge he has tried to give a sensation of movement to his static creations. The bison of Altamira, the Discobolus, baroque mythological themes, even the modern cinematographic art, all have tried to capture that coveted dynamism. The Lladró brothers have managed to make this centuries-long desire reality in their works of porcelain. The group representing four footballers achieves a plastic recreation of heated movement. Four players are seen in acrobatic postures attempting to reach the ball which the highest of the jumpers has managed to head. The violent foreshortening of each player and their forced postures make this piece a masterpiece of shaping technique.

The highest achievments of dynamism in porcelain would be incomplete whithout representations of an activity whose lightness and agility is beyond comparison: the dance. Two magnificent groups stand out from others in this field: a pair of classical ballerinas and a couple of flamenco dancers. Both examples display a perfect knowledge of both types of dance. The exquisite piece showing the classical

This study of football players is a remarkable example of force, activity and dynamism. The close-up, right, illustrates the violent foreshortenings with which the artist has tried to create a sensation of movement: an expressive interplay between arms and contorted hands.

Left: a masterfully balanced study of two ballerinas in which one of the dancers has her feet in the air, supported in this position by a join in her clothes and those of her partner. The artist has found the perfect solution to the problem of representing light movement. Below: the nobility of a pair of Flamenco dancers or bailaores.

ballerinas reveals a great mastery of the material in which it is created. Indeed it is by no means easy to represent the leaps of one of the ballerinas with neither of her feet touching the ground. The problem has been brilliantly solved by secretly joining the two dancers' flowing skirts.

The flamenco couple has been made following all the tenets of classical posture. The *bailaor* (male dancer) is standing in a stylized position with arms upraised; the *bailaora* (his woman companion) crouches on one knee with one arm in the air. The expressive movements of the hands correspond perfectly to those we have seen so many times in the flamenco *tablaos*.

Another of the pieces which best expresses dynamism is the one representing three gazelles in flight. The violent foreshortening, to which the author was forced to have recourse in order to depict the jumps of these agile animals, is admirably resolved. The animals' forced equilibrium would be impossible to express were it not for a profound knowledge of the strength of porcelain.

Another group seems to follow on from that of the fleeing gazelles: a magnificent hunting scene. It is one of the most beautiful representations of pure movement. The compelling attitude of the horsemen, the fieriness and nerve of the horses and the zeal of the

The magnificence of these gazelle's heads (upper detail) ranks equally with the fleetness of their hooves (detail on the right). The smooth musculature and the stylization of the bodies produce the illusion that these representations in porcelain are, in fact, alive, and the agility and grace so characteristic of these beasts has been admirably captured.

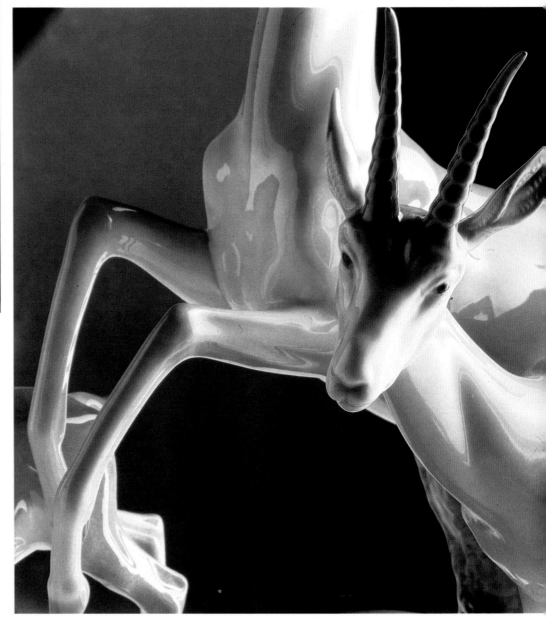

The swift career, the leaps and the agility of these Grant's gazelles have been remarkably captured in this piece.

Left: the close-up permits us to appreciate better this feeling of movement, visible particularly on the horses' manes and the rider's scarf. Below: the dogs tousle each other in the excitement of the chase.

Left: this hunting scene is undoubtedly one of the most successful porcelain studies of dynamism. Everything about it expresses movement: the fiery steeds, the tension of the riders and the speeding hound pack confer upon the piece all the excitement and colour of nineteenth-century hunts.

dogs endow the whole with an almost palpable vivacity. Every known recourse has been put to use here so that this fair-sized piece would have the final effect of a real hunt. The jumping motion of the horses has been cleverly exploited to disguise their means of support. The dogs pursue their quarry in a furious race. With the exception of the huntsmen's jackets we notice that only three colours have been used thoughout: brown, grey and green. This chromatic simplicity is offset by the blue and red of the imposing riding jackets. The fine coursers'

117

nostrils are dilated due to the speed of their chase and their manes billow in the wind. The group is one of the masterpieces to have come out of the Lladró factory.

Among all the terrestrial animals there is one which, by virtue of its beauty and agility, the elegance of its bearing and its centuries-old service to man, deserves special attention: the horse. The art of porcelain could in no way overlook the qualities of this magnificent animal in its search for ways to express dynamism. Rather than subordinate them to scenes which required their presence, it was decided to create groups with the expressed intention of exalting the horse's artistic possibilities. A particularly interesting example of this is the piece in which three wild horses appear, perhaps the best of all those dedicated to a single animal.

It shows three wild steeds in the middle of a fight: two of them rear up in a tussle while the third lies exhausted on the ground. The stylization of the forms serves to accentuate the violent postures in which they are caught. The modelling of two of the horses' bodies is impeccable in every detail: the fineness of the legs and their complicated positions, the form of the heads, the twisted tails, the long necks with waving manes, the spirited movements, etc.

The neutral colour and absence of varnish on this splendid piece do not mean that it its incomplete, but rather reflect a search for unusual perfection. Indeed the white colour reinforces notably the vigour of the forms by making their outline stand out with greater precision; the absence of varnish accentuates the texture of the piece making it rougher and less shiny, more precise and less delicate. The absence of colour and varnish confer a unique quality upon this piece.

Animals in Porcelain

These exquisite close-ups and the entire piece, which appears on the following page, allow us to appreciate the decorative exuberance of this study of flora and fauna.

Let us now abandon the world of galloping horses' hooves to enter the serene realm of the air to contemplate the repose of birds in flight. It is a world of animals of much smaller proportions which offers a microcosmos of immense dynamic possibilities.

In the works representing exotic birds the artists have managed successfully to combine flora and winged fauna. An exquisite example of this is the piece displaying two colourful birds in which the composition is based on an original idea: one bird stands with its wings outstretched, about to take off, on the top of a twisted tree-trunk, while its mate sits on the ground in readiness to follow.

Three colours predominate in this piece: green, brown and brownish yellows, while the most outstanding note is given by the red of the beaks, legs and tails. The intensity of each colour tone

contributes greatly to the attractiveness of the piece. Note, for example, the way in which the contrast between the green leaves and the dark brown of the trunk is heightened by the presence of the birds.

In the close-up we can see in greater detail the modelling of the birds' bodies, in this case that of the one perched on the trunk. In the foreground we are able to admire the intricate way in which the stoneware paste has been exploited to show the different kinds of feathers. Dynamism has been achieved fully through the open wings and the head which searches upwards for the road to follow. This is one of the most decorative stoneware pieces within the limits of the theme.

Still in the field of pieces uniting the world of birds to the world of flowers, but this time in porcelain, we encounter the following exquisite scene: two little

birds resting beside an exotic plant laden with white bell-flowers. The delicacy of the flowers blends perfectly with that of the birds.

One again we find ourselves before the fantastic world of porcelain flowers. The gentle, delicate colour of these harebells is heightened by the yellow of the pollen on the tip of the stamens and inside the calyces. The fleshy, tender stems are of a greenish-grey colour which contributes to the elegance of the whole. The enormous amount of work needed to make each flower —the bells were first made one by one and then attached to every stem— is eclipsed by the overall harmony of the piece.

The placid existence of these little birds is marvellously expressed in their attitudes: not only their having perched on this exquisite plant, but also their expressions and plumage all emanate peace; their gaze is curious and alert, yet trusting. Their plumage is completely at rest, displaying its tenuous colours. Absolute mastery has gone into the treatment of this theme based on a naturalist vocation revealing the harmonies of nature. The colour of the birds does not differ greatly from the colour of the soil in which the plant is growing, and in this way the coexistence between the animal and vegetable world is subtly suggested.

Another example of the importance of bird colouration in the world of porcelain is this original pair of ducks. We say original because the scene features two uncommon elements: in the first place it is one of the extremely rare pieces in which water not only appears, but also seems to be moving. The submerged beak of one of the ducks causes concentric ripples to form on its surface. The presence of water also allows for the presence in the piece of an unusual flower: the water lily. Five different techniques were used to colour this piece: the lily

was painted in the normal way but without glazing. Strong earth-based colours were used also and glazed after. The third technique was the usual one for painting porcelain, used in most of the pieces we have seen so far. Stoneware colouration was the fourth technique and liquid colouration the fifth.

In second place we notice the boldness of the composition. The duck which is about to alight on the water occupies considerable space in this posture. With its open wings and its feet in the air, the artist had no alternative but to support all the weight of the bird on its hindquarters, resting on the leaves. The uninitiated observer marvels at this single point of support: that such a small area should be abe to support both the weight and the imbalance of the exuberant duck seems little short of impossible. Only its creator can explain this display of virtuosity which has assured the piece a place among the best porcelain creations.

Another motive for special attention is the remarkable colour and showiness of these water birds. They are realistic examples of the species known as *coll vert* (green neck) found in the Valencian *albufera.* The female's plumage is mottled brown while the male has a green head and neck —hence the name—, brown and white plumage on the body and top end of the wings, and blue wing-tips.

During the last years of the seventeenth century and the beginning of the eighteenth, the constructive spirit of the baroque gradually began to disappear in favour of the pure ornamentation and decoration of rococo. Its most original exponent was A. Messonier, a noted Turin silversmith, considered by his contemporaries to be the real inventor of the specific forms of the new style. Its main characteristic was a tendency to overlook the exterior of buildings in order to concentrate attention on interiors and the

The scarcely sufficient support base of this duck with open wings is yet another demonstration of mastery in the use of porcelain.

Birds have always been a classical subject for porcelain. In the illustrations on the left we see these little winged creatures living in delicate harmony among exquisite flowers. Both the legacies from the orient and from romanticism, with its inspiration in nature, are elegantly represented here.

Two more fine examples of nature captured in porcelain can be seen here. Above: the charming contrast between the pink of the flowers and the bluish plumage of the little birds has been achieved with extraordinarily good taste. Left: this most interesting piece reunites the beauty of the vegetable kingdom and the animal kingdom in an exotically decorative study.

industrial arts. Basically French and German, it was in the decorative arts where it had most influence and where it achieved its greatest successes. Rococo was characterized by a prolific naturalism and a return to pastoral themes. The rococo style was particularly important in Valencia and can be seen in elements of interior decoration, such as the lamps in the Palacio del Marqués de las dos Aguas. This style favoured the development of porcelain.

Evidently the influence of this highly decorative and naturalist style can be seen in one or two of our porcelain works. The themes are varied but have one element in common, small birds perched on

exquisite flowers, and their most outstanding characteristic is colour. Violet shades are seen side by side with pinks, greens beside blues, all interpersed with different shades of brown. Variations on the same theme offer infinite choice of compositions: a blue and pink bird perches on a tree trunk; another perches calmly on a stone; a third can be seen beside a cactus; a branch acts as a perch for a fourth; three birds have landed in one group of plants while four have landed in another.

In every case the postures are the same, the birds are either resting or about to take off, and this detail reveals the artist's taste for naturalism.

Left: this piece, one of the best examples of colour combination, depicts how a pair of exquisite grebes with their curious crests merge with the surrounding vegetation. In this case a mixture of greens, blues, ochres and browns have been combined in the impressionist manner to produce the effect of mysterious shades. The way nature protects the grebe through camouflage is also masterfully shown here. The above close-up allows us to appreciate the posture of the female, incubating her eggs in the surety that her mate will stretch out his neck to warn of impending danger.

Returning to the stoneware pieces we find one which is outstanding for its rare chromatic unity: a pair of exotic grebes half-hidden among the foliage. This curiously crested pair is a future family: the mother sits patiently on the eggs while the father stretches out his neck, on the lookout for danger and ready to defend his unborn brood.

The composition of the previous piece is surpassed by another, depicting two storks. This study is perfectly modelled and the effect of the composition is admirably contrasted by the open wings of one of the birds against the stylized neck of the other, who seems to want to soar up into the heights.

Another two pieces together form a fine group: a pair of male and female doves. On the left, the male adopts an elegant pose with his tail open to attract the female while she, on the right, is in a more modest posture. The intention behind the piece is to exploit all the decorative possibilities of the natural world.

There is an animal which, noble, affectionate and faithful as it is, could not have been overlooked

This piece offers a masterful balance of composition. The open wings of one of the storks offset the vertical effect created by the other's fine neck. The latter bird seems to long for the heights only her mate can reach.

This decorative pair of doves is, in fact, a single group composed of two separate pieces. The male lifts its head and haughtily opens its tail in a mating-call. At the back of the female's head we see the characteristic swelling which distinguishes her sex. The simplicity of this study heightens its decorative value.

in these studies: the dog, man's best friend. Here we find two types: those that are small and playful, and the large guard dogs. A third type, the hunting dog, has already been seen earlier. Here the authors' intention is to pay homage to this faithful companion.

From this point of view it is worth mentioning two scenes with small, playful poodles. In one of them there is a pair with their litter suckling the mother's milk. The other is an amusing episode in which these animals sometimes evoke an almost human world: a pair of puppies play with a ball. This scene brings out, in a dynamic way, the loveableness of the little animals. The dogs enjoy themselves somewhat surprized by the elusive qualities of this ball. The colouration is simple: the almost violet colour of the dogs is offset by the combination of orange and white on the ball.

Alongside the movement suggested by the group of playing puppies we find the static nobility of a magnificent Great Dane, majestically stretched out on the ground. Its erect head and ears suggest movement in a much more difficult and subtle way by alerting us to its potentiality. The Great Dane is in dignified repose but we feel that at any moment it

130

Previous page, above right: the playfulness of little dogs is perfectly expressed in this scene, in which we can observe the surprise of these animals at the elusiveness of the orange and white ball with which they are playing. Another illustration presents us with a charming canine family scene in which a litter of puppies suckles tightly against the mother.

Left: this amusing little puppy is highly intrigued by the snail which dares to crawl up his leg. The artist has managed to capture the characteristic way in which dogs move their heads slightly to one side when they see something they do not quite understand. Below: the elegance of this Great Dane is enhanced by the dignity of its bearing.

could leap into action. The animal has been depicted in an elegant posture: he rests on his hind legs, his tail drawn in, his front paws crossed, his ears erect, the mouth closed, and his profound gaze reinforces the nobility of the raised head.

As the finishing touch to this gallery of animals, we find the beautiful spectacle of three doves. While two of them proudly open their smooth tail plumage, a third flutters above their heads. The composition is admirable: any heaviness which might have been suggested by the placing of the two doves in the lower part of the piece is eliminated by the graceful wing beat of the third, who seems to be trying to protect his companions beneath his wings. The attractive postures and the decorative arrangement combine to endow the composition with that spectacular beauty so characteristic of the animal world.

A Universe of Stylized Characters

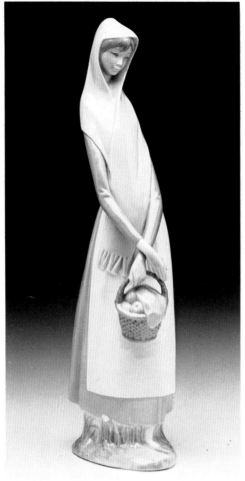

Left: the figure of the peasant girl, like those of the couple with the puppy and of the mother and son, on the following page, is simply designed, and its elegance is heightened by the stylization of form and serenity of the facial expressions.

The sternness of these two hunters returning home with their dog is compensated for by the elongation of their bodies. In this way an apparently unsuitable subject is converted into an ideal theme for a study in porcelain.

One of the most personal characteristics of the porcelainware under examination here is the elongation of figures, with the resulting stylization of forms. Slim bodies and tall statures are ideal for quotidian scenes since they raise them to the level of artistic themes: such is the case with the piece representing a mother contemplating her child or the scene depicting a lady playing with her little dog, watched over by her husband. These scenes, fundamentally so common, are the basis of small-object art. If porcelain is a witness of society and, consequently, a nexus of communication between different cultures, day-to-day scenes are the perfect vehicle for this purpose. In this sense the pair of hunters returning leisurely home accompanied by their faithful dog, or the young girl carrying a basket, reveal that the stylization of form can make any theme agreeable and pleasing, perfect for the decoration of the home.

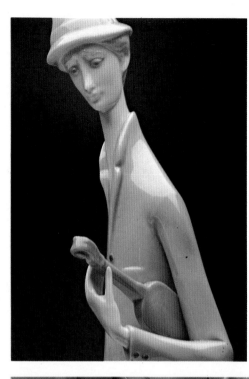

The romance
between this
vagabond
violinist and
the flower-
seller has been
depicted
through a
stylization of
form used
as a point
of contact
between the
characters and
the slender
tulips.

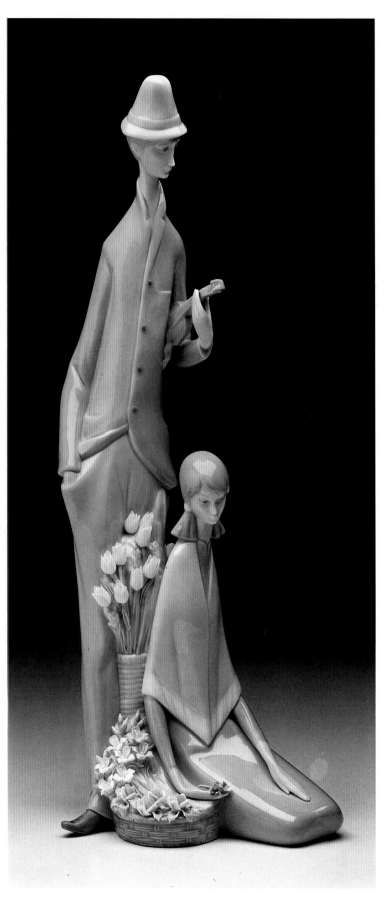

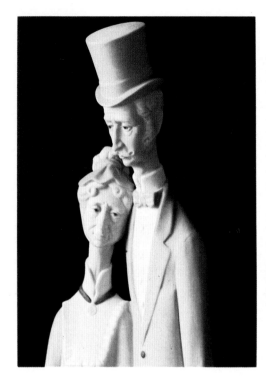

The humanity and sweet simplicity which emanate from old age have been admirably captured in the piece illustrated in the centre of the page. The stylization of profile symbolizes perfectly the serene mystery of those lives which the passing of years has converted into pure silhouette. On the right of the page: the innocence of the young girl holding up and contemplating her lap-dog has been captured through the slenderness of her body. This stylization of forms harmonizes in a special way with the expressions given to the faces, as the close-up so admirably shows.

The study of the two water-carriers is yet another example of the artist's mastery of modelling techniques and total self-confidence in the pursuit of his task. The necks, arms and busts of the two girls are just a glimpse of the pronounced stylization of their figures. Here once again we see the desire to depict a naïve and pacific world through the gentleness and elongation of forms. On the other hand the slenderness of the bodies accentuates the delicacy of these feminine figures. The composition is a study in visual balance, achieved by the proximity to each other of the two girls, one of whom has her arm around the other.

Through the stylization of forms the artist tries to flee from extremes to find refuge in middle terms, those gentle heartbeats which suit porcelain so perfectly. The admirable humanity and simple tenderness which emanate from age is perfectly expressed in the piece representing an old couple; the stylized profiles symbolize the mystery of these lives which the passing years have converted into mere silhouettes. The splendid youth of the two girl water carriers receives a special dream quality and delicacy with the stylization of their limbs and the gentleness of their gestures.

This sublimation of vertical forms is particularly ideal for those scenes evoking special tenderness: the young girl rocking a lamb, another arranging her friend's hair, yet another holding up her dog, as well as the pathos of the clown sunk in melancholy. The theme itself, that of a clown whose mission in life is to provoke laughter in others, in an attitude of dejection, is pathetic in itself; but the extreme slenderness and elongation of his outline accentuates the melancholy, rather than the grotesque aspect.

In reality the stylization of forms responds to a desire to give smoothness to lines, profiles and figures, in this way endowing them with a kind of innocence and removing any symptom of the prosaic.

Right: the title of this piece is The Coiffure, *and here again the artist has chosen to stylize the forms of these two adolescent girls in order to accentuate the innocence of their personalities. The piece above, representing the melancholy spirits of a clown, is worth mentioning apart. The sadness of a person dedicated to the provocation of laughter in others is deeply pathetic, but this has been softened here through the stylization of form.*

*The serenity which accompanies daily tasks, and which
we can admire both in the details and the entirety
of this study, reminds us of that poetic world evoked
by Santa Teresa de Jesús throughout her literary work.*

In other words, what we have here is an attempt to
transform what is crude and rough into delicate
harmonies and gentle outlines which evoke a world
of peace and tranquility. These effects are deliberately
sought since the artists are perfectly aware that
these pieces would otherwise find no place in the
intimacy of the home.

This voluntary deformation has for many
centuries been used by the artist to accentuate certain
aspects of his work. One of the most illustrative
examples of this stylization can be seen in the high
relief sculputes on the mullion at the main entrance
of Moissac Cathedral in France. These sculptures,
caught in a transition phase between romanesque and
Gothic, reveal the artist's intention to accentuate the
tortured spirituality of the protagonists through the
elongation of their figures; in the same way the
elongated outline of two stoneware nuns attempts to
emphasize the sublimation of the spirit in favour of
peace and an altruistic service beyond human
dimensions. The nuns' headdresses provide a masterly
balance to the otherwise purely vertical
composition.

Romanticism in Porcelain

Previous page: this is one of the most characteristic of the porcelain pieces evoking romanticism. The atmosphere has been admirably created: a stone urn, overflowing with plants and flowers, as in the most typical romantic gardens, a bench beneath the ample shade of a weeping willow, and the dress and parasols of the young women. Each element contributes to the recreation of that world of melancholy poetry.

This page: this study is another example of a delicate, romantic theme. Here appear two new and representative elements: the leafy arch, which serves as the backdrop to the scene, and the two little birds being fed by the girl. As in the previous piece, the theme here centres on the melancholy of maidens in love. The one represented here momentarily forgets her sorrows by immersing herself in her task.

Nineteenth-century romanticism is a veritable fountain of subject matter for porcelainware. Pastoral scenarios were those usually chosen by romantic authors on which to place their idyllic or melancholy scenes.

In this sense we have one piece which is an especially interesting example. It depicts a young couple, beneath a weeping willow, filling a basket of flowers. This scene contains all the typical elements of the style: parasols, the great stone vase of flowers from romantic gardens of the period, the bench, the flower basket, the weeping willow, a tree so suited to these scenes, and the characteristic clothes and expressions of the nineteenth century epoch. The

delicacy and good taste with which the theme has been treated here has kept it alive for the public of today.

One of the most suitable frames for any romantic scene is the one formed by a bench beneath a leafy archway. This is the backdrop to the scene in which a young seated girl with a dreamy expression contemplates and feeds a group of little birds.

Since the arrival of the first oriental porcelain works, European craftsmen have been inspired by the naturalism, between pastoral and romantic, with which they were decorated. As has already been said, porcelain, due to its delicacy and fragility, is the perfect medium for scenes of tenderness. The

Venice is the supreme example of that decadence so attractive to the romantic temperament; consequently the most authentic representative of exotic Venetian beauty, the gondola, could hardly be overlooked. No detail has been omitted which might contribute to that serenely enchanting atmosphere: the gondolier with his cape, the girl singing dreamlike melodies, and the pair of lovers.

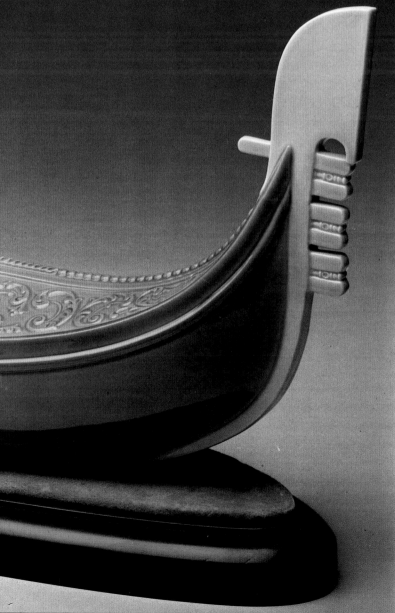

romanticism of last century introduced an enormous number of new themes into art: some sentimental, others of elegance and delicacy. The latter, direct heirs of the rococo style, have adapted most successfully to porcelain. The piece depicting a couple riding in a gondola is a perfect example. It is set suitably in the nineteenth century, and the attitude of the couple —listening intently to a little girl's song— harmonizes in a singular way with the vigorous gondolier. The gondolier himself, the prototype of all boatmen, is an absolutely romantic character —he belongs to the decadent world of exotic Venice— whose romanticism is here enhanced by the graceful cape.

Returning to wooded scenes, to leafy arches and pensive young people we find another perfectly representative study in which a young girl, leaning upon a balustrade, contemplates her little dog with indifference. The stylization of her figure and the detail of her clothes enhance the feeling of melancholy.

Another piece in the same style depicts a girl pulling petals off a daisy. Her reclining position and the bush in the background accentuate the bucolicism of the scene. The young girl's melancholy, as she consults the flower as to her loved one's true feelings, has been represented with a certain innocence and modesty.

A similar setting provides the backdrop for the famous scene of the swing. The romantic painting tradition always tended to use the most exuberant vegetation to accompany the innocent games of love-smitten maidens. This scene is reminiscent of the work of Watteau or Fragonard, and specifically that of the latter, among whose works there is a painting specifically entitled *The Swing.* Here also the swing is hung from the branch of a tree and the girl's dress is very similar to that of her counterpart in the work by the French painter.

In these types of scenes the trees invariably appear covered with exotic flowers and creepers, which endow them with the appearance of jungle

The four illustrations on these two pages, evoke that melancholy world romanticism so ideal for studies in porcelain. Previous page: a young girl stares absently at her little dog in a setting which contains three typically romantic elements: the leafy arcade, the balustrade and the parasol. Below: another typical scene in which a young girl consults a daisy about the true feelings of her lover. Right: a young woman rocking gently to and fro on a swing.

trees rather than those of woodlands; this is a typically romantic exaggeration. On the other hand, in the branches of these trees are perched tame little birds which, naturally, take us back into the world of the woods.

Oriental porcelain works which have reached the West are frequently decorated with mythological themes, treated in a purely decorative way as shown by those paintings on porcelain depicting complex, fiery dragons. This oriental approach left its mark in Europe, a good example being the nymph with her veils and hair blown gently by the wind, which responds to the romantic concept of mythological idealization. This is no goddess of Olympus but a nymph through which the artist has achieved

a most remarkable and original allegory of peace which was extremely difficult to model. Around the youthful figure, dressed in a classical, full-length, almost transparent tunic, and carrying a long veil waving in the breeze, we see a group of ethereal doves, since Biblical times associated with the concept of peace. If we look closely at the nymph we observe that in her left hand —the right hand from our point of view— she holds an olive-branch, that symbol of peace, hope and brotherhood with which the doves from Noah's arc announced a new era in the life of mankind to the weary travellers on that Old Testament voyage. The pale blue, so typical of Lladró porcelain, forms a gentle contrast with the pale flesh-colour

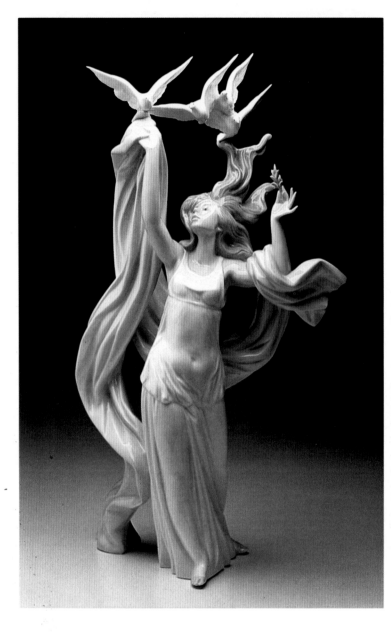

of the nymph's face and hands. This simple combination of two colours only confers upon the piece a sense of harmony endows it with a very special ethereal quality.

In the close-up on the right we can contemplate the skilful work of the sculptor in the composition based around the feminine figure and the space created by the position of her arms, the long, flowing tresses of her hair, and the abundant folds of her tunic and veil. This series of spaces and volumes is crowned by the delicate doves which seem to hover, almost weightlessly, above the nymph's head. It is hardly surprising that this piece, so painstakingly and dexterously modelled, should have become so extraordinarily successful and so sought after by art lovers in general and collectors of decorative porcelain in particular.

Inspiration in Literature

Previous page: romanticism and the literary and musical tradition meet in this study. The melancholy world of persistant but unrequited love is evoked by this bust of a troubadour. The famous Verona couple, Romeo and Juliet, also fall within the category of literary and romantic themes. Here Juliet's modesty and Romeo's air of the woman-conqueror have been expressed with elegance.

The exceptional half-length figure of the troubadour takes us back to the romantic world where music becomes a vehicle for human sentiment, where songs contain the most beautiful poetry dedicated to the loved one and where love itself is expressed through literature and music. This fine representation of a young, handsome troubadour exploits all the artistic possibilities of stoneware. Love's melancholy, as we know it thanks to traditions and literature, is expressed here in all its intimate beauty. Once again the artist has turned to the innocence and purity of youth to offer us this image which expresses masterfully the delicacy if the lyrical sentiment.

The hair gently blown by the wind, the well formed hands of the musician, his complicated costume, his dreamy pose and the colour scheme based on a range of ochres, red-browns and maroons gives the piece a notable unity. We are witnessing a dream world where young troubadours let the hours go by singing captivating melodies beneath the windows of their fair damsels who are beyond reach.

The literary grandeur of William Shakespeare has also found its place in the world of porcelain. If porcelain is suited to the intimate, homely world, Shakespeare's theatre is an eminently renaissance art, that is, an art which concentrates attention on human problems and the intimacy of this world. An idea so admirably profound and close to our hearts could hardly be overlooked when the time came to search for themes suitable for porcelainware.

The idyll of Romeo and Juliet is a piece which admirably expresses the love theme. The young girl displays simultaneously the desire and the modesty of a nascent love wich will eventually lead to total surrender.

This typicaly romantic scene is completed by the

Hamlet's famous monologue addressed to Yorick's skull is included in this gallery of literary figures. The doubt of Shakespeare's immortal character is clearly visible on his face in this porcelain study. The anxiety which tortures the young man's soul is reflected in his posture, while his intense eyes gaze into the depths of the skull seeking there the reply to his dilemma.

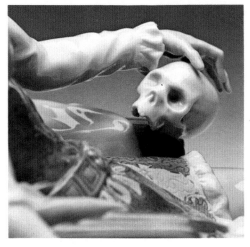

This piece is a variation of the one before. Now the Prince of Denmark is sitting on his unstable throne while delivering the monologue. His left hand rests on the bare skull (see close-up, above) while the prince tries in vain to find a satisfactory answer.

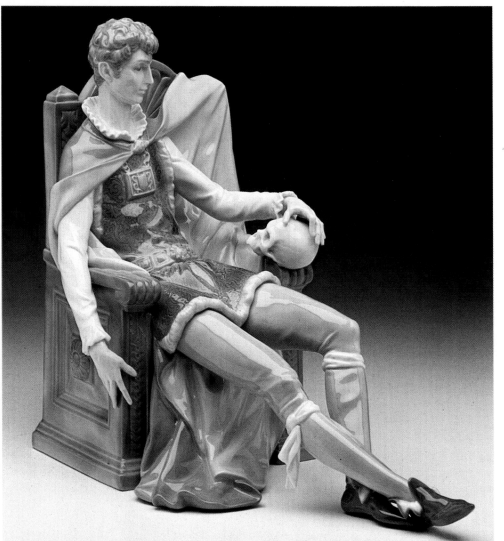

152

Another famous subject has been treated in this piece: Othello's jealousy of his wife, Desdemona. Shakespeare's classicism is revealed by the way in which neither protagonist shows outward signs of emotion.

stretch of wall upon which the audacious and lovesick Romeo sits. At the foot of the wall grow some flowering bushes, mute witnesses of the intimate encounter. The stylization of the protagonists responds to the desire to sublimate a motif which, being so commonplace, has been raised to the category of the unique by the masterful pen of the great poet and playwright.

The diversity of Shakespeare's work permits the discovery of innumerable themes suitable for representation in procelain. In the illustrations we see three of the most famous: Romeo and Juliet, Othello and Desdemona, and Hamlet. Two postures of the Prince of Denmark illustrate the treatment which the artist's genius has given the theme of Hamlet. Naturally the scene chosen is the famous monologue with Yorick's skull. In both pieces Hamlet holds the skull in his left hand while his gaze tries to pull a response from it which will resolve his doubt. With an evident desire to smooth passions, the author

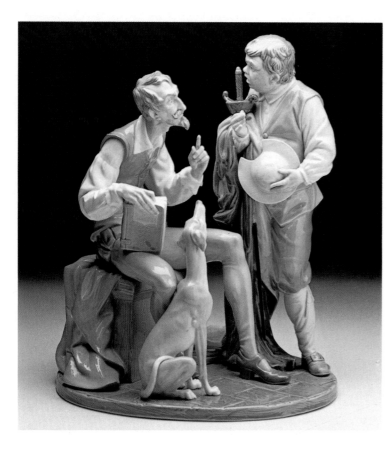

Don Quixote, in an attitude of repose belied only by the fanaticism which his tense facial expression shows, instructs Sancho in the arduous tasks of errant chivalry.

has managed to express Hamlet's anguish without any contorted expressions, limiting himself to gesture, pose and ambience to depict a human problem whose only solution is human also. The intense dramatic effect of the Shakespearian monologue finds its perfect complement here in the throne or the ruinous remains upon which the doubting prince lies, in the historic costumes and the forlorn postures.

The piece depicting Othello and Desdemona shows us the latter on a divan, disturbed by her husband's attack of jealousy. Shakespeare's classicism has been magnificently expressed here; Desdemona shows no terror, as she would have done if the romantics had depicted her, and Othello himself is controlled. Both of them contain their emotions, giving only slight indications of what is happening inside: she places her hand on her breast in a gesture of fright whilst her face displays no emotion; he leans over her in a menacing way but his

hand caresses, rather than grabs, his wife. The intention in capturing the great scenes of Shakespearian theatre for porcelain is to bring closer to us a world which, though of great depth, is not out of the reach of the majority. Through these little works any one of us can possess the beauty and charm of great masterpieces.

No less grandiose is the figure of that *ingenioso hidalgo* Don Quixote of La Mancha, featured also in the gallery of literary personages, as we can appreciate when we examine the three scenes, each one of which represents a different episode from the book. In one of them we see Don Quixote writing in one of this rare moments of calm and lucidity. Another scene depicts the gentleman whose desire was to die sane and live as a madman, sitting exhausted with one of the novels of chivalry, which poisoned his mind, on his knees. This piece has become considered the most representative of all the collections and has consequently acquired a just and merited fame. His elongated figure, dress and aspect correspond perfectly to the way in which Cervantes himself described him to us: 'Our hidalgo was just touching the age of fifty years: he was severe of complexion, dry of flesh, haggard of face, a great early riser and lover of the hunt (...) he gave himself over to the reading of novels of chivalry with such avidity that he neglected the exercise of the hunt and the administrarion of his estate; and such became his curiosity and folly in this matter that he sold many acres of cultivable land in order to buy novels of chivalry in which to read, and thus he brought to his house every available one of its kind.''

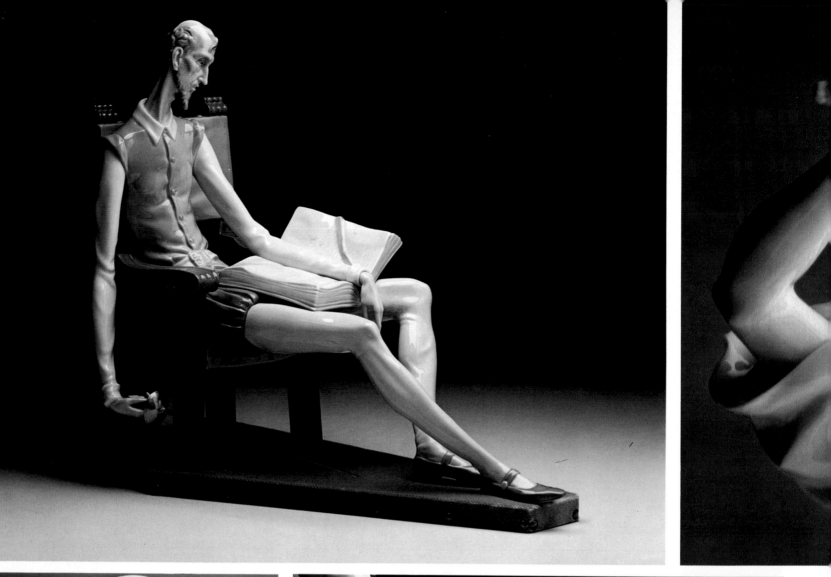

These pages: two excellent images of the famous hidalgo Don Quixote de la Mancha. Above: this scene is one of the most famous in the world of porcelain and one of the most representative of the novel: Don Quixote is seen reading the novels of chivalry which poisoned his mind so. His stylized figure serves here to heighten the idealism which Cervantes' hero professed. The close-ups of this piece reveal the perfect modelling. Right: this scene is, if anything, even more skilfully executed. It depicts our hero's fight against the wine skins, which he believes to be giants. The fury on his face is exactly that which the author ascribed to his protagonist in this hilarious moment of the novel. The hero's anatomy has been treated with particular care, especially his arm, and leg and hand muscles, while his clothing contributes greatly to the sensation of movement.

Another amusing and admirably constructed piece depicts a scene which has captured the Lladró brothers' imagination: the "Battle of the Wineskins". "Whereupon they heard loud noises coming from the cellars and Don Quixote's voice shouting", "Stop, thief, rogue, coward! For I have you here and your scimitar will be of no avail!" And it seemed as if he were striking out against the walls. Then said Sancho, "Do not stand there gaping but go in and stop the fight or assist my master; although there will be no need for you can be sure the giant is now dead and giving account to God of the evils of his past life; for I saw his blood running along the floor and his severed head, which is the size of a great wineskin, lying on one side." "May I be struck down", said the innkeeper at this point, "if Don Quixote or Sir Devil has not run through one of my skins full of red wine above his bedhead, and the spilled wine is what appears to this fine fellow to be blood."

Don Quixote searched for adventure all over the Spanish territory, and this gave the author an excuse to sing the praises of each region he passed through. The homage which the Lladró brothers pay to our hero and his creator is made from clays which

This little boy, dressed as Harlequin, takes us into the world of the Commedia dell'Arte. *This ancient theatrical tradition with its archetypal characters has been cultivated through the centuries, by all the arts. Porcelain is naturally an ideal material with which to represent this world of puppets. The close-up above reveals the innocent face of this little boy tenderly hugging his cat.*

158

the hidalgo could quite easily have trodden in his exploits. It is a homage to an immortal personage or an act of justice intelligently carried out.

This series of figures taken from literature would not have been complete without representatives from that secular world of rich theatrical tradition: the Commedia dell' Arte. This tradition is founded on the very essence of theatre: to capture the audience's attention through intrigue created on the stage. It is the world of fairground performances featuring those character archetypes so intimately related to the masks of ancient Attic theatre. Columbine, Pierrot, and Harlequin are the three figures from the Commedia dell' Arte for which the Lladró brothers have felt a special preference. It is no coincidence that these should be precisely the subjects chosen since they are the ideal ones to reflect that romantic, infantile and pure world which is so suited to porcelain.

The youth of the seated boy harmonizes perfectly with the Harlequin costume he is wearing. This piece evokes the blue period of that genius from Málaga, Pablo Picasso. This little boy's sweet gaze is the very essence of naïveté, melancholy and infantile peace. His dangling legs complete this so personal vision which the author sought to confer upon the piece. The chromatic unity —blues and whites— is admirable and gives a smooth harmony to the whole, from which the light touches of pink detract in no way whatsoever.

The beautiful love scene between Columbine and Harlequin reminds us of the other similar scene between Pierrot and the ballerina. Here the stylization resolves the problems of the absolute delicacy with which Harlequin must treat Columbine, and the result is a veritable embodiment of the subtlety of porcelain. The coquettishness of the ballerina has been expressed in a most delicate way: rather than demostrate her fickleness the artist has accentuated the femininity of her figure. Harlequin's hands and gestures reveal his great gifts as a conqueror of women.

The study of Columbine at rest is an excellently worked piece combining dynamism with delicacy and purity of form. Columbine is seated and immobile but her graceful posture makes us imagine her in the full flight of a dance. On her face we can still see the

The theme of the idyll between Columbine and Harlequin is, without a doubt, one of the most apt to be represented in porcelain. This delicate romance has been depicted through the postures and gestures of the protagonists: the figures have been stylized, the arrangement of legs, arms and hands has been carefully studied, and the faces have been endowed with great expressiveness. The tenderness with which Harlequin caresses his beloved Columbine is most moving.

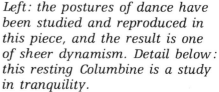

concentration with which only a few moments ago she carried out her movements. It seems that her delicate body was born for the dance and can only express itself through this medium. Note the brilliant way in which the artist has achived the delicate folds in her skirt.

Mythology is another indispensable element in this gallery of fictional characters, but its treatment should be prudently restrained if it is to be suitable for porcelain. It is true that the most attractive themes of classical mythology are those which refer to the great divinities: Saturn, father of all the gods; Jupiter, the most powerful; Neptune, king of the seas; Mars, god of war or Mercury, the winged messenger; without forgetting the beauty of Venus, the skill of Diana, the strength of Minerva or the astuteness of Juno. However, these gods cannot be separated from their power, which means that if they are to be represented plastically, their size must be in keeping with their might and splendour. Neptune, Venus and Mercury were thus represented during the renaissance. One cannot countenance these themes in the world of porcelain.

However there is another marvellous world which accompanies the life of the great divinities and which is as full of fantastic and beautiful detail perfectly expressible in porcelain. The artists dedicated to porcelain have exploited this thematic vein: two mythological fantasies belonging to the world of metamorphosis, namely, the centaur and the siren.

Below: three figures which belong to the fantastic and esoteric world of the sirens, represented here with women's torsos and fish's tails. Their juvenile and waving bodies constitute yet more studies of the feminine figure.

While the former fuses the virile human torso with the muscular body of a horse, the latter is an admirable and delicate combination of feminine body and fish's tail. Both mythological forms are the perfect expression of masculinity and femininity respectively.

The group of four sirens captures our attention thanks to the detail of the rocks on which the marine numphs are seated, the wave and their windblown hair. This group is among those which best express the idea of movement: it is almost as if the sirens were making every effort possible not to fall into the sea.

The world of porcelain is not suited to strong

features, or severe or suggestive forms; it prefers warm themes, gentle forms, simple characters and innocence free of all suggestiveness. The representation of sirens and centaurs had to join the mythological theme with simplicity and ingenuosness: and youth was the key. Consequently we observe the total success of the piece representing two child centaurs —she with that innocent modesty of youth and he with the sauciness typical of small boys— which, through a delicate range of brown colours and amusing postures, manages to capture our hearts. These pieces cannot help but remind us of the good taste and genius with which Disney made his film Fantasia.

Left: two small pieces which reflect a deep knowledge of the infant soul. The boy centaur yawns and stretches with the cheekiness characteristic of a boy his age, while the girl centaur covers herself, somewhat ashamedly, in a typically feminine posture. Right: close-up of the sirens from the previous page, in which we can appreciate the perfection of the faces and the graceful bodies of these mythological creatures.

A Serene Devotion

The details which appear on this page show us the brilliant modelling of the most difficult parts of the human body to represent: the face and the hands. The expressiveness which has been given to this Virgin with dove is completed by the perfection of finish. This is doubtlessly one of the best made faces, particularly in the way the Virgin's serene gaze is captured.

The vast Spanish religious tradition has, for many centuries, been the inspiration for innumerable works of art. Painters, sculptors, image-makers, architects and decorators have all dedicated a large proportion of their output to religious themes; and now the Lladró brothers have revived this tradition through the media of porcelain and stoneware. When it was decided to incorporate religious subjects into this world, the imagistic heritage must have carried most weight since it is a very rich Spanish tradition which has been expressed in a number of ways, from Gothic and Romanesque sculptures and reliefs to woodcuts in the same styles; from stone and wood renaissance imagery to baroque religious themes; from the Catalan Nativity tradition to the ancient and solemn Andalusian Holy Week processions with their pomp and stateliness. This long tradition could by no means be overlooked and the Lladró brothers have adapted it to their own style.

One fine piece bears a marked resemblance to the woodcut of the Virgin of Cracow. She is a virgin who, despite her erect posture, unites the peace of her features with that of the resting dove. The composition is based on curved forms: the wavy hair, the hands forming an oval and the baroque swirls of the shawl.

The Nativity tradition has also been given a place here. Another beautiful scene depicts the manger and, if only the Holy Family appears here, there also exists a large collection of pieces representing the shepherds and the Three Kings to complete the scene.

Right: the lengthy image tradition of Spain is represented by this Virgin with dove. Perhaps the most characteristic legacy of that tradition is the swirl of the cloak, which adds an extraordinary element of dynamics to the piece. Stoneware gives added presence to the piece.

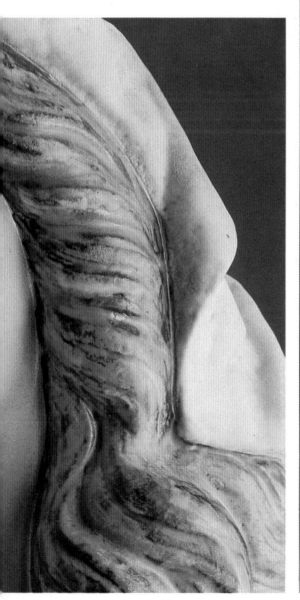

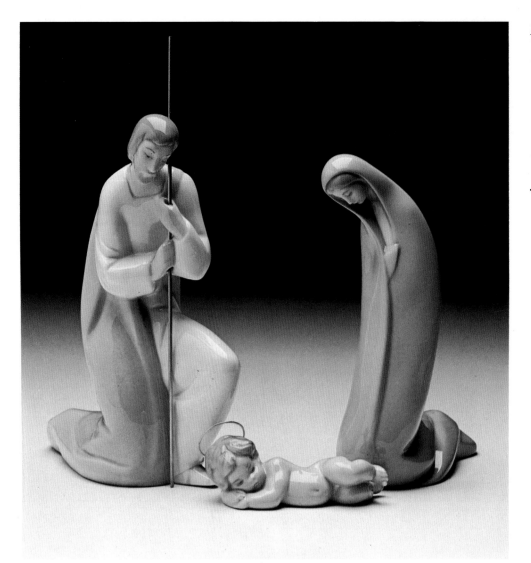

Two different aspects, one traditional, postures, and the other modern, form, have been made to meet in this piece. Joseph and the Child have been modelled more or less classically, but the Virgin has been conceived in a highly original way. She is, without any doubt whatsoever, the most striking example of stylization of all Lladró figures. The simplicity of the group prevents the observer's eyes from wandering from the scene itself.

The already-mentioned legacy of religious images as well as the importance placed on scenes from daily life are combined now in the representation of Santa Teresa de Jesús. She was a woman of tremendous energy who eventually became famous as the founder of the Order of Discalced Carmelites and innumerable convents to serve the order. She was almost obsessed with domestic details; her attentions in the kitchen, her concern for cleanliness and daily chores were the basis of her life and faith. Even in her literary works she frequently mentions domestic tasks in great detail. This world of apparent trivialities and routine is an ideal subject for porcelain, and our artists have paid tribute to it in their portrait of the saint who saw "God among the pots".

The piece representing Saint Teresa admirably expreses her serene devotion and her deep understanding of religious mysticism. The nun from Avila appears seated and relaxed, writing the words which her divine inspiration dictated. Colours gently contrast with each other, the saint's attitude and expression are very telling and the atmosphere gives off a feeling of quiet seclusion. That magic which from earliest times has been embodied in small figures as propitiators of forces deeply rooted in man's conscience here finds its loveliest manifestation.

The colour and texture of stoneware have been magnificently exploited in the piece depicting the Virgin and Child, a figure highly reminiscent of the medieval image tradition which cultivated this theme to a great extent. The gentle curve of the Virgin's stylized body serves a double purpose here: to increase the sense of unity —the Child rests heavily on his mother's hip— and to dispel any effect of rigidity. The faces of Mother and Child and their clothes are

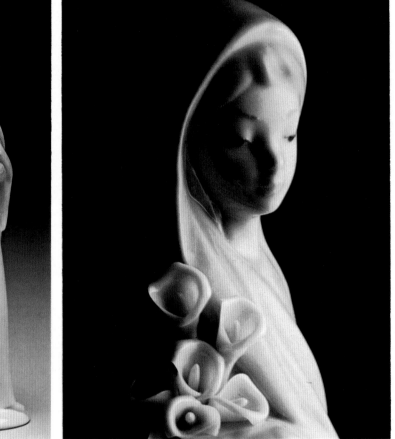

traditional elements which have merited special attention here. Indeed the complex cloth out of which the Virgin's robe is made is reminiscent of the robes of similar medieval Virgins, just as the happy faces and postures remind us of those ancient woodcuts.

In another piece a young girl appears who could easily be a Saint or a Virgin because of her mystical expression and the lovely bouquet of calla lilies she is carrying, doubtlessly as an offering. This small piece is modelled with extreme delicacy.

One aspect of the long religious image and painting traditions is the one which depicts tiny angels in the scenes representing the Virgin, Jesus Christ or the Saints. These delicate creatures accompany the pious personages with their games and celestial music. The Lladró brothers were attracted to this subject and one of the results is a scene in which three angels sing from a score. This is a humanized vision of these spiritual creatures, represented as if they were real children. The six little angels in

The illustrations on these two pages reveal the artist's considerable skill as a modeller both in porcelain and in stoneware. The magnificent Virgin with Child, extreme left, the young girl with lilies, left, and the groups of little angels on this page all delight us with their irresistible charm.

another piece are —as in the case of the little girls making up or the others with their straw hats— variations on the same theme. Every possible posture and all the different instruments have been modelled with unsurpassable mastery.

A subject with a very ancient tradition, especially in Spain, is that of the Three Kings who came from the Orient to worship the Child, and the group of three pieces stands out immediately from among the religious works. This group became famous for reasons other than its unquestionable artistic merit. Once made, the Lladró brothers decided to present it to the then current Pope, Paul VI, who gladly accepted the gift. Later, when the first three

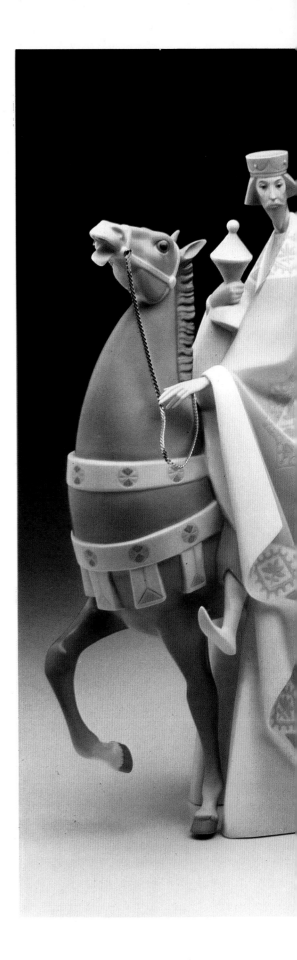

American astronauts to set foot on the moon visited the Vatican, His Holiness gave them a King each as a souvenir of the visit, underlining the similarity between the first space travelers and those oriental Kings who, according to tradition, were astronomers. Upon learning of this gesture, the Lladró brothers made another, identical group and offered it once again to the Pope.

The group constitutes an especially personal interpretation of the theme. On examining the three pieces we become aware of two things: the traditionality of the theme and the modernity of its treatment. First we notice its conventional aspects: Melchior, Gaspar and Balthasar bring their gifts of gold, frankincense and myrrh, riding majestically on their mounts. However, then we become aware of the artist's original mode of design where he uses angular lines as if wishing to communicate the vigour and haughtiness of the royal personages. The foreshortening of the fiery steeds accentuates this sense of the power of their masters, while the riders' serenity enhances their air of wisdom. The dignified postures, firm attitudes, sobriety of dress and the spirit of the horses all combine to endow these sages with a notable strength of personality.

The subtle shades are combined in the most harmonious way; blended creams, pale blues and immaculate white being the only colours used. Only the golden reins and the slightly pink colour of the little coffer and one of the King's trousers depart from the predominant chromatic range.

The horses are worth mentioning apart. They substitute the legendary camels as the monarchs' mounts and they are agile, arrogant beasts who seem eager to break into a full gallop; their alert and restless heads, their ample, muscular necks, their strong, pawing hooves and their nervous tails are

The three close-ups on this page reveal three fundamental aspects: modelling, design and expression, on the group of the Three Wise Kings. The heads of the fiery horses are perfectly finished and comparable to the precise design of the hand, and the serene countenance below this text.

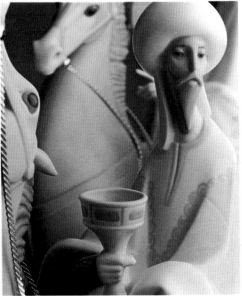

masterful embodiments of dynamism and suggest the store of energy contained within these magnificent animals.

The contained prepotency, which this marvellous group suggests, in no way prevents it from being suitable for porcelain. It is a lesson in the mastery of modelling techniques in which power and decorativeness are joined in a harmonious whole. The pieces are glossed rather than glazed and their perfection makes them a worthy gift for the Head of the Catholic Church.

An Immortal Legacy: the Genius of Orient

Left: the exotic beauty of this piece is a direct result of the oriental legacy. The postures of these two Balinese dancers are an example of an original concept of integration of figure and space.

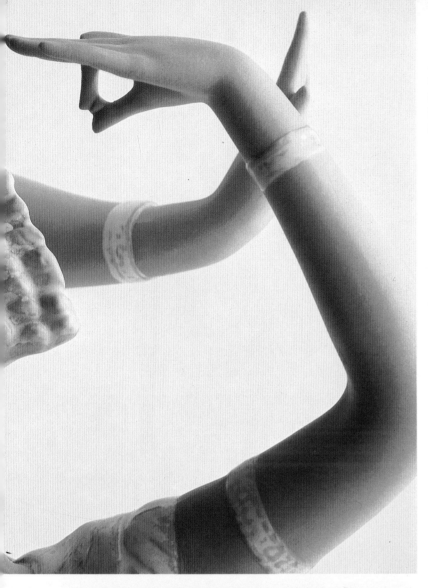

Left and below left: in these two close-ups we can appreciate the delicate and intricate interplay of the stylized positions of arms, hands and fingers, and the spaces created between them which become as much a part of the composition as the figures themselves.

A fundamental concept of oriental philosophies is to be close to Nature and the harmonies which emanate from her. This gave rise, in China, to the Palace of Supreme Harmony and porcelainware, to the famous Japanese rock gardens with their miniature tree species, to the tiny Hindu altars for the worship of their divinities and to the complicated costumes for Thai dances.

Concern for detail and for smallness and domesticity led to styles as wide ranging as the baroque of Hindu art and the sobriety of Chinese or Japanese landscapes. Both styles were reflected in porcelain; the former on the great vases with their complicated and coloured dragons, while the latter has traditionally been associated with landscapes and flowers painted on to porcelain works.

Turning now to the work of our present-day craftsmen, the Indonesian ballerinas illustrated here are an example of the oriental heritage, visible in the vivid colours and the marked contrasts. The lively colouration, the delicate postures, the effect of harmonious movement, the concentration on the dancers' faces and the overall chromatic harmony confer upon this piece a beauty which reflects the technical virtuosity of its creator. Its undeniably decorative qualities, on the other hand, make it one the most interesting of the oriental-type pieces.

Only one other figure can stand comparison with the previous one in terms of beauty and technical skill: the pair of dancers, in typical costume and headgear, performing a Thai dance. This scene is a feast of colour, of interplay between hands and feet, effects of movement and costume detail, as if the artist had delighted in the difficult process of expressing with skill and apparent simplicity the highly complex postures of the dancers' bodies.

composition is gentler, more delicate even. The innocence of the facial expressions is heightened by the headdresses and contradicted by the coquettish interplay of fans and feminine kimonos. Colours here recover their former restraint and angular forms have become rounded in the search for the best possible composition.

The world of the geishas has been converted into a world of innocence, just as the world of mythology was, through the use of childlike faces and ingenuous expressions. From among all the oriental pieces one in particular stands out: the young geisha kneeling and arranging a flower vase. This little masterpiece has become exceptionally successful, particularly in the United States. This is no coincidence since the principal enemies of the United States during the Second World War were the Japanese, and the fight against them took many American servicemen to Japan for a period of time. There they came into contact with the geishas, who came to represent a haven of peace, in the post-war period and after the horrors of war itself, which those soldiers would never forget. Consequently American war veterans are particularly attracted to this piece. The delicate whites, greys and blues combine with the gentle pink of the flowers, while one element only provides a necessary note of contrast: the warm brown of the little table.

This dance study is a perfect example of dynamism, to such an extent that we almost see these young Thai girls swaying to the rhythm of the music. Empty spaces have here also been incorporated into the composition of the piece, while decorative fancy has been exploited to combine colour with movement.

Right: these four Japanese women are dressed in the typical kimono, while two traditional elements complete the creation of atmosphere: the fan and the parasol. Their postures express classical Japanese attitudes: the dance and the greeting. All four women are moving, as we can see from the slight flexion of the legs. What we are seeing, in face, is the same ballerina observed at different moments, and the four figures together constitute a kind of film sequence, frame by frame.

178

To left and right of the central illustration we see a closer view of the modelling of these porcelain figures. The flowers in the hair, the slightly oblique eyes, the hardly noticeable nose and the small lips give form to these so infantile Japanese faces. The position of the hands and fingers has been given special attention, both where they hold a fan or a parasol and where they make a smooth gesture inherent in the dance they are performing.

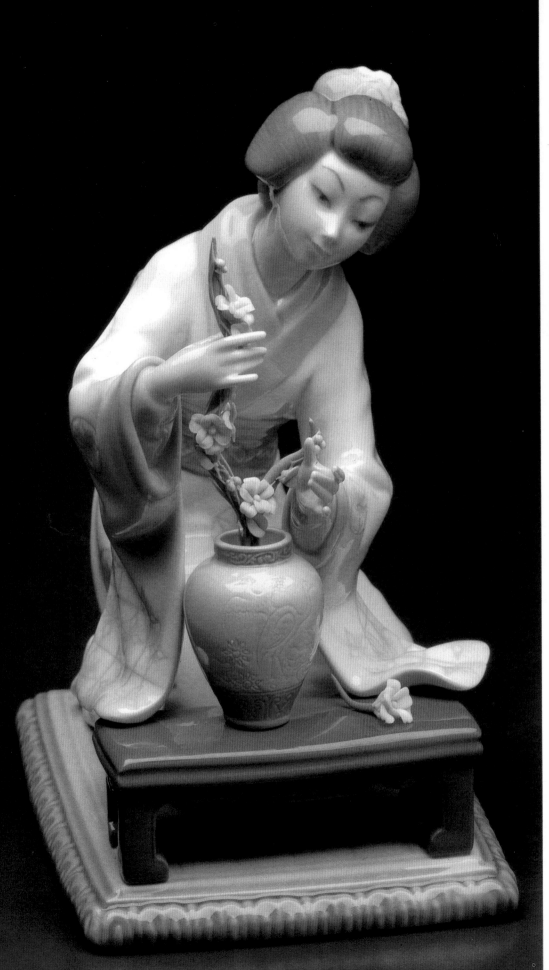

The marvellous close-up below reveals the perfection with which each hand was modelled. The fingers were made separately in order to produce the illusion of graceful movement. The extreme simplicity of the flowers harmonizes with that of the hands.

The little figure on the left represents a geisha in the act of preparing a floral decoration, arranging flowers in a vase. Both its size and its true-to-life quality make this a veritable work of art.

The Modesty of Nudes

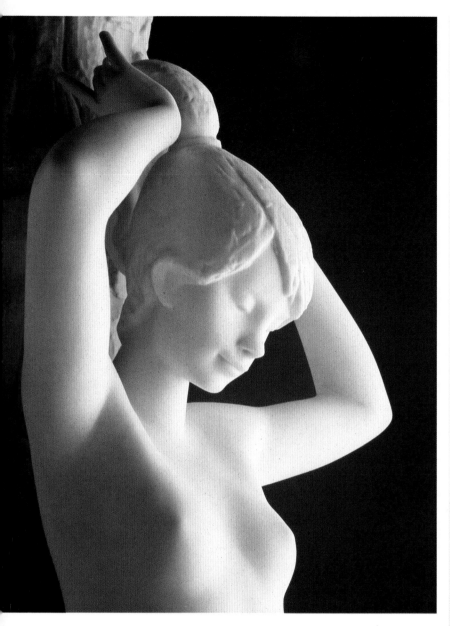

The beauty of the feminine body has traditionally been one of the themes most cultivated by every art form; but in the case of Lladró porcelain and stoneware the sensitivity of the creator, given the qualities of those materials, had to find ways to deprive the nude figure of any hint of provocativeness.

Above all he had to accentuate the ideal delicacy of youth and the morphological purity of the adolescent body. In second place he had to endow nude figures with a sensuality —which is totally unavoidable in this case— full nevertheless of modesty and innocence. This has been achieved in a piece depicting a subject which, since time immemorial, has

This group of the Three Graces is an excellent study of the nude figure. Each of the Graces is in a different position. The main problem in depicting a nude figure —anatomical perfection— has here been resolved without difficulty, since we can see that the artist possesses
a deep knowledge of the characteristics of porcelain and how they can be exploited to shape nude figures.
The texture of unglazed porcelain has also been made use of here to create the effect of human skin.

been used to represent the forms of the feminine body: The Three Graces. A highly personal aesthetic vision has transformed the originally young but developed Graces into three charming adolescents. Once again the artist has resorted to the absence of colour, and the unconcerned postures of the three girls respond to the purity of their natures. In order to enhance their innocence they have been represented with their eyes closed; in this way their intimacy remains uninterrupted and undesecrated by the outside world.

Another example, perhaps the most beautiful of all that could have been chosen, is the one which links

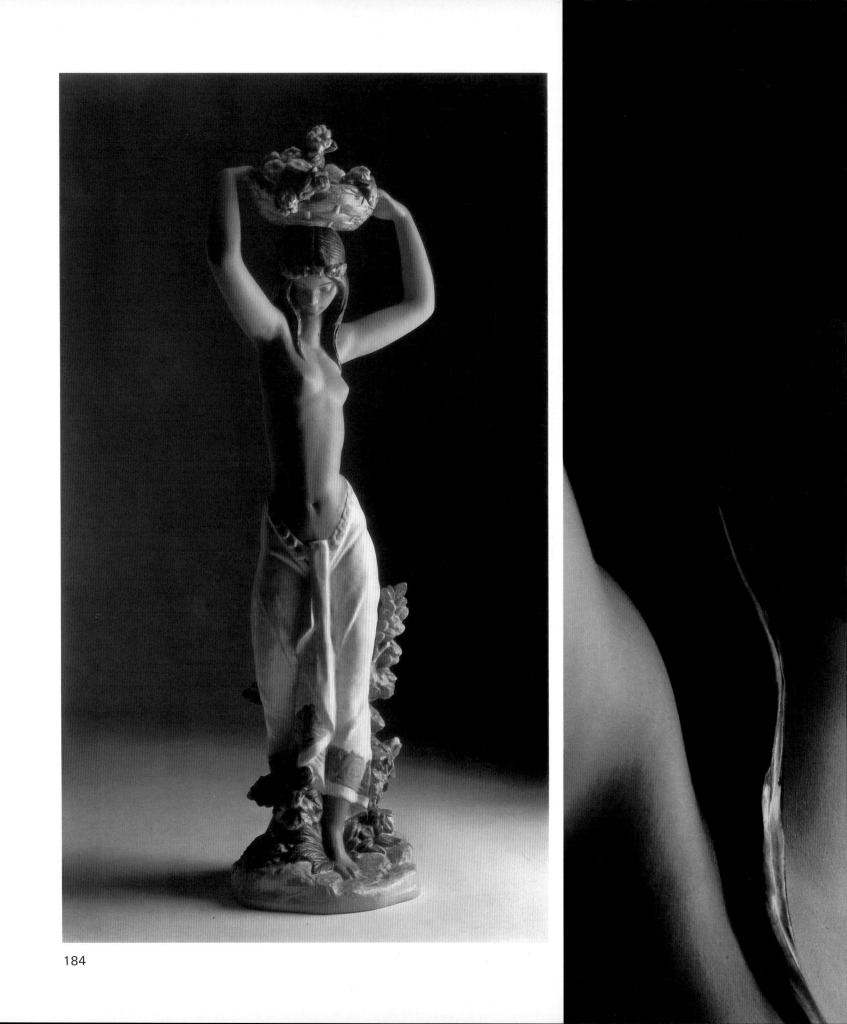

The illustrations on these two
pages show one of the most
beautiful Lladró nude studies.
The main characteristic of this
young girl is naturalness:
her body, the bush and the basket
of fruits all participate in the
purity of natural things.
Her slightly twisted trunk
heightens the elasticity of the
body, while the position of her
arms responds to a desire to
give balance to the composition.
The central close-up reveals the
perfection of the face and the
innocent expression, while above
we see details of the basket of
fruits and the girl's hair.

185

the nude figure to the world of daily tasks, thus confering upon the naked body a perfect naturalness. The girl's expression reflects that inner security which is the fruit of innocence, and the perfect union between feminine body, basket, and thicket enhances this effect: the foliage is as natural and as innocent as the fruits and the figure which carries them. The composition is yet another example of mastery; and its verticality calls one's the attention to two things: the slight contortion of the body and the openness of the arms holding the basket, both of which add great interest to the whole. The skilful way in which the piece was modelled is enhanced by the presence of colour.

A further example of the nude figure is the one which represents an adolescent leaning against a three. The artist has deliberately created the impression that the piece is incomplete the better to heighten the beauty of this highly stylized feminine body. The absence of colour, apart from the light brown of the tree trunk, prevents the observer's attention from straying from the girl's exquisite figure, so masterfully modelled that no colour was needed since it could add nothing to the innate beauty of adolescent bodies.

This piece is a striking example of how the artist has achieved a feeling of total innocence, removing all suggestion of provocativeness. Note, in particular, her downward, demure expression, recalling the timidity of the little girls seen earlier, dressed up in their lavish costumes, and the posture of her left hand which clutches the robe gently, as if fearing that it may fall and leave her body totally exposed.

Porcelain in the Service of Games and Design

These illustrations reveal that this chess game is a successful incursion into the world of practical objects.

The influence which the Far East had on porcelainware was not limited to purely decorative forms but also looked for ways of expressing itself within the world of useful objects. The ancient game of chess —and here we recall the *Treatise on the Game of Chess* by Alfonso X The Wise— is believed to be a Chinese invention. The Arabs introduced it into Europe when they occupied most of the Iberian Peninsula. This game of intelligence, based on the rules of strategy, was originally composed of figures representing the principal participants in a battle: the supreme command (the monarchs), the cavalry, the assault towers, the royal guard and the infantry corps.

The close-ups of the chess set
show each one of the six
different pieces during a game
in progress. This arrangement of
pieces permits us better to
appreciate the decorativeness of
the set as a whole. It is here given
a medieval setting as a
reflection of the time-old
Spanish chess tradition,
first described in Alfonso X
the Wise's Treatise on the
Game of Chess, which appeared in
the thirteenth century. Though
keeping to the classical form
of each piece, this set
nevertheless has a personal
feel expressed through the facial
expressions and the treatment of
costume.

The treatment which the lampstands have received (above and left) bears a direct relationship to their function. A pruned tree constitutes the support column for the bulb and the shade. Idyllic scenes have been chosen to comply with the verticality of the pieces: two different versions of the romance between Harlequin and Columbine. Left: the two figures are combined on the same stand. Above: two separate stands with a figure each form a set.

However the original coincidence between each piece's function and its representation was gradually lost in the West, until the pieces themselves became abstract symbols.

On making the chess pieces in porcelain, the craftsmen bore the original function of each one very much in mind. The costume of monarchs and vassals chosen was that of the time of the wise king and essayist, Alfonso, in order to heighten the

Spanish character of this game which has been played here for just under one thousand years. There are six different pieces for each side: King, Queen, Bishop, Rook, Knight and Pawn. The pieces have not been given a lavish, baroque appearance but rather a simple *mise en scène* based on rounded forms and shaded colours. Black and White have been distinguished by a deepening of the tones on the pieces representing Black.

Staying for a while within this world of useful objects, represented by the magnificent chess game, we come across lampstands decorated with pastoral and romantic scenes.

Here we offer two fine examples in which Harlequin and Columbine live out their idyll through music and dance. The pruned tree which appears in each one of these pastoral models here functions as the main support column. The theme has been given an ethereal and delicate treatment to adapt it to the decorative and the utilitarian.

This incursion into the field reserved for industrial design has, proven to be absolutely successful,

and has responded to a desire for greater personalization of these objects whose specific function need not necessarily isolate them from the intimacy and warmth of the home.

The absolute mastery with which oriental craftsmen made their vases has obliged porcelain manufacturers to create pieces worthy of the legacy left behind by that difficult art. Traditionally the reputation of a porcelain factory has rested on the quality of its vases. In the case of the Lladró factory, what seemed impossible has been achieved, and it is now situated among the manufacturers of the most beautiful vases in the world.

The variety of forms and decorations of the vases reveals a highly refined style and extraordinarily good taste, of which we offer here an extensive sample. Within these variations, every vase has been designed to suit the themes and colours decorating it. Thus we can contemplate a wide-bellied vase with a bell-shaped neck, decorated entirely in relief. Exotic leaves and flowers contrast with the little birds perched among them. The principal colours are

It has long been thought that vases were the most difficult objects to make with beauty and elegance, since they were derived from an oriental tradition which was

extremely rich in this field. Nevertheless the vases illustrated here are among the most sought-after in the world. It is easy to understand this if we examine the one on the left.

blues, gentle violets, greys and whites. The bell shaped neck of this vase is substituted, in another fine example, by a subtle cylindrical form which complements the pronounced and profusely decorated belly. We see a tree whose silhouette is dressed with a mosaic of pale, intelligently arranged autumn leaves. In the centre of the picture is a magnificent peacock. The rich colouration is contrasted by the delicate light background, and in this way the piece acquires equilibrium.

We can also admire four beautiful vases of two different designs which form two pairs by virtue of their decoration. In the ones on the right the form is stylized and the decoration includes peacocks and other exotic fowl perched on the branches of rare flowering trees. This paradisiacal scene is the perfect vehicle for its creators to show off their virtuosity in the application of colour. The chromatic contrasts stand out against the background and create an almost musical harmony.

In these illustrations we can admire the variety of forms and decorations of these vases. Some have bulging bellies while others are slenderer and more agile in form. On some the necks are elongated and on others shortened to keep in proportion with the whole; some are bell-shaped while others maintain the sobriety of cylindrical shapes. Peacocks vie with no less exotic birds for supremacy in elegance while the most spectacular flowers imaginable combine with whole varieties of different leaves. The colour contrasts stand out against the backgrounds, creating almost musical harmonies.

The two close-ups on this double page reveal the care which went into the making of these little birds, perched on tiny branches or shoots.

This pair of vases is an excellent example of mastery of form and decoration in this field. The brilliant design detracts in no way from the elegant sobriety of the vases.

Other examples are somewhat less stylized than the previous ones but their decoration is of greater subtlety. In one a pair of little birds has perched on the twisted branches of a flowering tree; in the other another pair of birds clings to tiny stalks emerging from a pond. In both cases the precision of the design and the delicacy of the colours combine with the shape of the vase to achieve an elegant balance. Once this difficult technique has been mastered, any porcelain manufacturer can rest assured that he has passed the last and most involved test of maturity.

Throughout this book we have had occasion to discover the evolution of the art of porcelain from its remotest beginnings in the Far East and its rediscovery in Europe during the eighteenth century, to the heights of artistic achievements and popular success which Lladró porcelain has reached in our times.

Above all the work is marked by the presence of three brothers who have made the miracle possible thanks to their professionality and will to work. But it is no less true that this objective was achieved also through the endeavour and enthusiasm of a team of technicians, sculptors, painters and a whole host of other collaborators imbued with a profound sense of common cause.

We have seen the wide spectrum of themes which decorative porcelainware covers, and whose plastic representation is made possible through the application of different treatments and techniques. The subjects range from the most trivial daily occurrences, passing through the world of romanticism and of the animal kingdom, to exotic scenes and religious figures and groups. The Lladró style, so easily recognized and yet so difficult to define, cannot be explained simply in terms of colour, or the stylization of figures, or even the perfection in the finish of every piece. It is something which exudes from each creation and which establishes a point of contact between artist and observer.

Pastes, colours, shades and forms, in other words, technique and art, are joined in exquisite compositions which embellish these pages, and the book as a whole offers a choice selection of Lladró creations. As in the case of the best European manufactures of the past, the works and style of Lladró are contemplated with admiration and respect by all those dedicated to the field of artistic porcelain, and the extraordinary width of their diffusion over the five continents has earned Spanish porcelain a well-deserved and world-famous reputation.

*   *   *

When we come to the end of this work which, like a magic kaleidoscope of shapes and colours, has offered us a whole panorama of beauty and harmony, we realize that these two admirable aesthetic values can be reached by following a straightforward and uncomplicated path: that of simplicity.

Simplicity and creative integrity have indeed walked hand in hand throughout this journey into the wide world of porcelain. We have found nothing ostentatious; nothing outrageously striking has perturbed us, shattering our tranquillity as we read or upsetting our peaceful contemplation. We have been able to admire the most divers subjects and a gallery of different personages; yet within this indisputable variety the common denominator of simplicity has prevailed, and at each instant we have felt the presence of that supreme ingredient, indispensable to all works of art: the love injected into everything which is made, everything which is created.

This love and this simplicity are plainly given form in any one of the compositions we have contemplated, in each of the gestures and attitudes of the figures, in each of the thousand different colour variations. As can be seen, the predominant tones are mauves, pinks, lilacs, ivories; and only very occasionally do we come across lips of a gentle carmine or the subdued glow of a red flower.

And all this framed by a world which communicates pleasure and happiness to us. A world of innocent illusions and beautiful sentiments. A world, moreover, which appears before our eyes as something past and wonderful. The examination of these porcelain works transports us in spirit a few centuries back in time when beauty and elegance were not only aesthetic values, but one could even say vital, essential qualities for acceptance and self-furtherance in a society which at the time believed itself to be secure and indestructible. It was the world of unforgettable eighteenth-century creations at Sèvres, Meissen, and Buen Retiro: the charming shepherds and shepherdesses with their fine hands and aristocratic mannerisms; the willowy-figured ladies with powdered wigs who seem to have stepped out of that rococo court over which Marie Antoinette presided.

A world, in short, which though it seems to belong to us no longer, has been evoked and recreated by Lladró with such skill that it has been given new life and its constant and inalterable presence assured for all time.